MW00466886

BOGIE TALES OF EAST ANGLIA

A Victorian folklore collection

M. H. James

with an introduction
by

Francis Young

First published as *Bogie Tales of East Anglia* by Pawsey & Hayes, Ipswich in 1891

First published 2019
St Jurmin Press
Peterborough, United Kingdom

A catalogue record for this book is available from the British Library

ISBN 978-0-9926404-6-0

Contents

Introduction

Francis Young

I encountered M. H. James's *Bogie Tales of East Anglia* by accident, during the course of research for my book *Suffolk Fairylore* (2018). My first reaction was surprise that I had never heard of the book. Published in 1891, *Bogie Tales* was the first book dedicated to the folklore of Suffolk and Norfolk. Yet it has faded into obscurity – such obscurity, in fact, that it seems only a handful of copies survive. Throughout the twentieth century, no subsequent work on East Anglian folklore cited James's book, although one author, Morley Adams, plundered *Bogie Tales* without offering any recognition to its author.[1] As a result of Adams's plagiarism some tales from James's book have made their way (sometimes in garbled form) into later collections of East Anglian folklore, but the book and its author have remained almost completely unknown. Until now, *Bogie Tales* has never been reprinted.

Not only is *Bogie Tales of East Anglia* the first book dedicated to East Anglian folklore, but its author Margaret Helen James (1859–1938) was the cousin of one of the best-known East Anglian authors of the late nineteenth and early twentieth centuries, Montague Rhodes James, and the sister of the pioneering librarian Minnie Stewart Rhodes James. In 2017, research by Andrew Lohrum and Rosemary Pardoe confirmed

---

[1] Adams, M., *In the Footsteps of Borrow and Fitzgerald* (London: Jarrold and Sons, 1914).

the identity of Margaret James as the author of *Bogie Tales.*[2] Although its title might suggest that it is a work of supernatural fiction, *Bogie Tales* is in fact a collection of highly localised folklore, primarily from the eastern Waveney Valley and the Suffolk coast, especially the seaside town of Aldeburgh, collected by Margaret James herself and an unnamed male collaborator whom she mentions in the preface.

M. H. James

Until recently, the identity of M. H. James was a mystery, and the subject of some strange theories. Writing in 2002, the M. R. James scholar Rosemary Pardoe rejected the suggestion that 'M. H. James' was a collective pseudonym adopted by M. R. James and his brother Herbert Ellison James,[3] but noted that a 'Miss M. H. James' was credited by M. R. James with compiling the index to his book *Suffolk and Norfolk* in 1930.[4] In 2017 Andrew Lohrum encountered an obituary for Margaret Helen James in the journal of the Alpine Club that unambiguously identifies her as the author of *Bogie Tales* and as a cousin of M. R. James:

> We regret to announce the death from pneumonia on December 9, 1938, of Miss MARGARET HELEN JAMES, who for many years has compiled the index for the *Alpine Journal.* Miss James was well known to many of the leading publishers, who entrusted to her the compiling of indexes for their more important publications on travel, history, memoirs, biography,

---

[2] Pardoe, R., 'Miss M. H. James, author of *Bogie Tales of East Anglia*', *The Ghosts & Scholars M. R. James Newsletter* 31 (April, 2017), p. 32.

[3] Pardoe, R., 'Queries', *The Ghosts & Scholars M. R. James Newsletter* 1 (March, 2002), online edition, users.globalnet.co.uk/~pardos/GSNews1.html, accessed 16 February 2019.

[4] James, M. R., *Suffolk and Norfolk: A Perambulation of the Two Counties with Notices of Their History and Their Ancient Buildings* (London: J. M. Dent, 1930), p. vii.

> medicine, congress reports, etc. This work, on which Miss James was engaged for a period of at least forty years, invariably won praise for its accuracy and completeness. She possessed two assets of great value to her in her work: a wide knowledge, and a really brilliant memory. Among the more recent indexes for which she was responsible have been, her cousin the late Dr. Montague Rhodes James's *Suffolk and Norfolk*, her friend Dame Millicent Fawcett's *What I Remember*, *Marlborough* by Winston Churchill, and *The Jews in the Modern World* by Dr. Ruppin. Miss James also published a collection of stories called *Bogie Tales of East Anglia*. To a remarkably retentive memory and an almost encyclopaedic knowledge of East Anglia, was added a zest for reading, and she was possessed of a charming personality.[5]

Pardoe and Lohrum were also able to establish that Margaret Helen James was a daughter of Henry Haughton James (1827–85),[6] one of six full brothers of M. R. James's father Herbert James (1822–1909) (there was also a sister and two half-brothers). Henry Haughton James was a commander in the Indian Navy before becoming a coal merchant and maltster in Woodbridge, Suffolk. His first wife, Sophia Helen Courthope, died in 1866 and he remarried Annie Say Sparkes (1839–1909) in 1867. Minnie Stewart Rhodes James (1865–1903), Henry Haughton James's second daughter with his first wife, became a leading librarian and the foremost advocate of women librarians in the late nineteenth century.[7] The 1881 Census reveals that Margaret Helen James, born at Elham, Kent in 1859, was Minnie James's elder sister. In 1881 a twenty-two year-old Margaret

---

[5] Quoted in Pardoe (2017), p. 32.

[6] Ibid.

[7] Perrone, F. H., 'James, Minnie Stewart Rhodes (1863–1903)', *Oxford Dictionary of National Biography*, online edition, doi.org/10.1093/ref:odnb/59735, accessed 17 February 2019.

James was living in Cumberland Street, Woodbridge with her father, stepmother, two brothers and two sisters.[8]

In *Bogie Tales*, Margaret James tells us that three of the tales were already published elsewhere. She tells us that she personally investigated folklore 'belonging to the villages between Beccles and Bungay, on the Norfolk side of the River Waveney', while some other material in the volume was collected by a male collaborator. Her brief preface and introduction explain James's approach to folklore collection; some of the tales were simply remembered from her own childhood, but 'most of them were gathered from the lips of entirely illiterate people, who for a long while had no suspicion that what they told was to be published'. James reports that the idea of publication put many of her informants off, either because they suspected James of not believing them, or because they considered publishing the tales unlucky. Karl Bell, the sole author to have considered Margaret James as a folklorist, has suggested that this suspicion on the part of her informants reflected a reluctance to allow oral traditions to pass into a print culture that might expose them to ridicule by 'anonymous readers'. James's informants perceived the supernatural entities of their tales as 'a constant and very real presence that would be aware of their transition from an oral account to a literary tale'.[9]

In addition to acknowledging the reluctance of some of her informants, James also acknowledged the limits of her collection: 'The collection is not presented as being in any sense exhaustive, and, indeed, only touches the fringe of what is, doubtless, a very mine of folk-lore'. She again uses a mining metaphor when she notes that her collaborator 'was fortunate in striking a hitherto unworked vein of folk-lore', and that she

---

[8] The National Archives, Kew: *Census Returns of England and Wales, 1881*, fol. 108, p. 25 (digitised at ancestry.co.uk, accessed 22 February 2019).

[9] Bell, K., *The Magical Imagination: Magic and Modernity in Urban England, 1780–1914* (Cambridge: Cambridge University Press, 2012), p. 145.

found 'an almost undiscovered lode in the rich mines of folk-lore' in the Waveney Valley. James's choice of metaphor is not insignificant; nineteenth-century folklorists often perceived folklore as a fixed deposit, laid down centuries ago, much like precious metal or gems in a mine. As James herself claims in her introduction, 'unwritten tradition survives quite marvellously, until people learn to read'.

Folklorists have long since distanced themselves from such a view; in reality, folklore is constantly evolving because it is continuously informed by print culture, and customs and tales are often not as ancient and immemorial as they appear to be. James grasped, however, that folklore may evolve, suggesting that 'the spirit is maintained amongst the people which will actually develop fresh supernatural beliefs in this prosaic century'. This was a rather unusual suggestion for the time, when the emphasis was normally placed on the decline of folklore and the need to preserve the remnants of a dying tradition.

The title

The title of *Bogie Tales of East Anglia* is, in some respects, a strange one. 'Bogie' is not a distinctively East Anglian word, but the term and its variants (such as 'bug', 'bogle' and 'bug-a-boo') are used throughout Britain to refer to any frightening supernatural being.[10] However, only the first thirteen tales feature 'bogies'; the remaining seven do not even feature a supernatural element, and are instead local anecdotes about eccentric characters and tragic events – elaborated, in some cases, at considerable length.

There are two main ways of explaining this discrepancy. The first possibility is that M. H. James began writing a book about encounters with frightening supernatural beings and then ran out of time or material. She then either chose, or was

---

[10] Briggs, K. (ed.), *An Encyclopedia of Fairies: Hobgoblins, Brownies, Bogies, and other Supernatural Creatures*, 2nd edn (New York: Pantheon, 1976), p. 30.

encouraged by her publisher, to add additional tales to make up the length of the book, including material she had already published in magazines. James reveals in the preface that three of the tales were already in print, and although I have been unable to trace them to any periodical, it seems likely that they included the last two tales, 'The Beach King' and 'Geordie, the Sea-waif' on the grounds that these tales are longer than any of the others and show signs of extensive literary elaboration that do not appear elsewhere in the volume.

A second possibility that might explain the book's uneven subject matter and slightly misleading title is that James initially intended the book as a serious folklore collection, but her publisher exerted pressure on her to present it as something more sensational, perhaps encouraging her to choose a title that promised frightening supernatural content. James's aspirations as a serious folklorist are clear from the preface and introduction, but the book's original front cover (featuring a highly stylised and somewhat sensational ghost) suggests that Pawsey & Hayes tried to market the book as a 'penny dreadful'. If they did so, they were evidently not successful, and the book's rarity may be an indication that the print run was small, or that unsold copies were pulped.

The publisher's attempt to sell folklore as supernatural fiction may have been a transitional phase in Pawsey & Hayes's move to becoming a publisher of serious folklore two years later, when they printed Lady Eveline Camilla Gurdon's collection of Suffolk folklore for the Folklore Society.[11] Because the title *Bogie Tales of East Anglia* is not truly descriptive of the book's content and potentially misleading (because it might lead some readers to

---

[11] Gurdon, E. C. (ed.), *County Folk-lore Printed Extracts No. 2: Suffolk* (Ipswich: Pawsey and Hayes for The Folklore Society, 1893). On the history of Pawsey & Hayes see Watson, S. F., 'Some Materials for a History of Printing and Publishing in Ipswich', *Proceedings of the Suffolk Institute of Archaeology and History* 24 (1948), pp. 182–227, at p. 213.

believe the book is a collection of supernatural fiction), for this edition I have added the explanatory subtitle 'A Victorian folklore collection'.

Reception of the book

The original publishers' attempt to market the book as sensational literature may have had an adverse impact on the reception of *Bogie Tales of East Anglia*, at a time when serious studies of regional folklore were coming into vogue. Under the heading 'Folk-Tales and Songs', *Bogie Tales* was listed in the Folklore Society's bibliography of books published in 1891,[12] but it appears to have attracted no further notice over the next twenty years. Even Eveline Gurdon, whose 1893 study of Suffolk folklore was brought out by the same publisher as *Bogie Tales*, gives no indication that she was aware of the work of M. H. James (although, to be fair to Gurdon, her collection of Suffolk folklore was probably completed before the publication of James's book). The neglect of James's work may have owed something to the fact that (unlike Gurdon) she was not a member of the Folklore Society; she also lacked Gurdon's social prestige as a member of the landed gentry.

Unfortunately, the earliest author to take notice of James's *Bogie Tales* did so by plagiarising them. Much material from *Bogie Tales* appears in the pages of Morley Adams's book *In the Footsteps of Borrow and Fitzgerald* (1914), entirely uncredited, and sometimes presented as oral tradition collected by Adams himself. Since Adams's book is well-known and James's is not, much of the material collected by James has been attributed to Morley Adams by subsequent folklorists, including by Jacqueline Simpson and Jennifer Westwood in their vast compendium of

---

[12] 'Folk-Lore Bibliography', *Folklore* 2:3 (September 1891), pp. 394–400, at p. 394.

regional folklore *The Lore of the Land* (2005).[13] Indeed, Adams's plagiarism has gone unnoticed until now. Among the few authors to have noticed M. H. James are Kirsty Hartsiotis, whose *Suffolk Folk Tales* (2013) includes a version of James's 'A Were-dog Story' under the title 'The Italian',[14] and Karl Bell.[15]

Bogie Tales of East Anglia is undoubtedly an imperfect book; like many early works of folklore, its author struggled to find a coherent structure by which to organise it, and her decision to make 'bogies' the central theme of a book that is not really just about frightening apparitions may have been a mistake. Most problematically of all, James's reluctance to name many of the places and people she writes about, and her use of fictitious names, presents significant challenges in making use of *Bogie Tales* as a source of folklore; I have attempted to identify as many of the places alluded to in the text as possible, but I have not always been able to do so. Yet this ill-assorted miscellany remains the earliest book on East Anglian folklore, and many traditions were recorded for the first time in its pages – however they were subsequently misappropriated by Morley Adams.

Margaret James richly deserves the credit that has hitherto been denied her as a pioneering East Anglian folklorist, not least because *Bogie Tales of East Anglia* stands out as a folklore collection in which women's voices are to the fore, including the voices of ordinary rural women. Tale 1 ('Lucky Chance') is told from the point of view of the witch of Loddon's daughter; many of James's informants were women, and James chose to tell the stories of two eccentric women alongside the three odd squires who feature in the volume (Tales 17 and 18, 'Miss Waterton' and 'Mary Broom').

---

[13] Westwood, J., and Simpson, J., *The Lore of the Land: A Guide to England's Legends, from Spring-Heeled Jack to the Witches of Warboys* (London: Penguin, 2005), pp. 499–502; 688; 693–4.

[14] Hartsiotis, K., *Suffolk Folk Tales* (Stroud: The History Press, 2013), pp. 98–103.

[15] Bell (2012), pp. 145; 187 n. 90.

Perhaps the most harrowing tale in the volume is Tale 19, 'The Beach King', which has no supernatural elements and instead focuses on the tragedy of a young woman sold into marriage by her father in payment of a debt. It is not hard to see the tale as Margaret James's indictment of a society in which a woman under twenty-one years of age could still be forced to marry under the terms of a legally watertight contract. Even in Tale 19, 'Geordie, the Sea-Waif', the woman who takes Geordie in from the sea is arguably as significant a character as Geordie himself. Together with her friendship with the Suffragist leader Millicent Garrett Fawcett (who was born in Aldeburgh), mentioned in James's 1939 obituary, James's approach to women's voices and experiences in *Bogie Tales* suggests that she may have been a self-conscious feminist.

The tales

Bogie Tales can be divided into two broad sections. Tales 1–13 are examples of supernatural folklore, including non-narrative collections of miscellaneous lore such as Tale 10 ('Charms and Cures'). The second half of the book (Tales 14–20) consists of non-supernatural tales reporting local eccentrics of the late eighteenth and early nineteenth centuries (Tales 14–18) and local tragedies (Tales 19 and 20). As I have already noted, the book's organisation is haphazard, but since the Folklore Society was only in the earliest stages of establishing norms for the writing of regional folklore studies at the time *Bogie Tales* was published, it is difficult to be very critical of M. H. James for her arrangement of her material.

The book opens with a tale about witchcraft: the story of a witch's daughter in Loddon, Norfolk who manages to escape the fate of inheriting her mother's supernatural powers. The belief that witchcraft was inherited was especially prevalent in East Anglia, as was belief in imps (witch's familiars, usually in animal form).[16] At Horseheath in Cambridgeshire it was believed in the early twentieth century that the village witch had to pass on her imps to a relative before she could die. One witch at West Wickham tried to burn the box containing her inherited imps, only to suffer burns on her own body while the imps were unharmed, and as late as 1926 a local newspaper reported that the imps of the witch of Horseheath were delivered to a relative after she died.[17] Although the witch of Loddon also features in Morley Adams's *In the Footsteps of Borrow and Fitzgerald*, on this occasion his version of the story is sufficiently different to make it plausible that he really did hear it from an 'old lady … particularly well up in the local history of witchcraft',[18] rather than plagiarising it from James.

Tale 2, 'The Hateful Thing', features a curious shape-shifting creature that could only be seen by certain people. In a footnote, James drew attention to the fact that the creature went into Geldeston churchyard, and connected it with the 'church beast' or 'Church Grim', the spirit of a black dog that was deliberately killed in order to protect a churchyard from the devil, and has Scandinavian origins.[19] This tale was plagiarised by Adams,[20] as was Tale 3, 'Ghosts on Wheels', which focuses on spectres of the Bigod family borne in a ghostly coach around Bungay, as well as the regular apparition of a hearse at Spixworth in Norfolk.[21] Tale 4, 'Goblin Ground', returns to Geldeston to describe other ghostly phenomena, including the ghost of a man whose chained skeleton was found under a millstone at the

---

16 On belief in imps in East Anglia see Young, F., *Suffolk Fairylore* (Norwich: Lasse Press, 2018), pp. 67–75.

17 Porter, E., *Cambridgeshire Customs and Folklore* (London: Routledge and Kegan Paul, 1969), p. 164.

18 Adams (1914), pp. 44–6.

19 Westwood and Simpson (2005), p. 502.

20 Adams (1914), pp. 190–1.

21 Ibid. pp. 193–5.

bottom of a drained pond; this part of the tale found its way into Adams.[22]

Tale 6, 'A Were-dog Story', was told among Lowestoft beachmen and features a mysterious Italian visitor who can shape-shift into a large black dog. The tale was borrowed by Adams,[23] although Adams's failure to identify Lowestoft as the location of the legend led to subsequent divergence of opinion among folklorists (none of whom were aware of James's original tale) about where along the East Anglian coast the incident should be placed. As Peter Tolhurst has observed, folklorists attempted to associate the legend with locations as diverse as Lowestoft, Cromer and Felixstowe.[24] Kirsty Hartsiotis was the first folklorist to make use of James's original and therefore to place the action in its correct location of Lowestoft.[25]

Tale 7, 'The Wild Boy', takes an ancient Suffolk tale from the Middle Ages and relocates the action in the late eighteenth century, with some adaptations. James noted that the tale 'may be found in a very old guide-book, long since out of print, [and] is also, sometimes, referred to King John's reign'. The original story is that of the wild man of Orford, recorded by Ralph of Coggeshall in the early thirteenth century.[26] The guidebook in question may have been the 1870 edition of *Murray's Handbook* for Suffolk, which alluded to a 'tradition' of the wild man of Orford still existing in the village.[27] In James's version the original wild man is replaced with a boy, who is discovered not at sea but in the marshes. This was another tale plundered by

---

[22] Ibid. p. 195.

[23] Ibid. pp. 126–8.

[24] Tolhurst, P., *This Hollow Land: Aspects of Norfolk Folklore* (Norwich: Black Dog Books, 2018), p. 191.

[25] Hartsiotis (2013), p. 98.

[26] Ralph of Coggeshall, *Radulphi de Coggeshall Chronicon Anglicanum,* ed. J. Stevenson (Her Majesty's Stationery Office: London, 1875), pp. 117–18.

[27] Murray, J. (ed.), *Handbook for Essex, Suffolk, Norfolk and Cambridgeshire* (London: John Murray, 1870), p. 149.

Morley Adams, who somewhat eccentrically viewed the wild boy as an embodiment of Shuck.[28]

The tale merges elements of Ralph of Coggeshall's narrative with events from the life of the historical 'Peter the Wild Boy', a boy found in the woods near Hanover in 1725 and brought to the court of George I.[29] For example, the wild boy refuses to wear clothes and becomes angry when he sees them, and refuses to learn to speak. The villagers intend to present the wild boy to the king and baptize him 'George', but the boy is unwilling to learn to behave like other human beings and is condemned to a menial task. Like the wild man of Orford, the boy is taken to the governor of the castle, hung upside down by his feet, and allowed to play in the sea under supervision; and like his medieval predecessor, the wild boy eventually escapes. The coda to the tale in which 'a certain kind of vetch' becomes mysteriously edible after the wild boy's departure, during a famine, derives from a report by William Camden. In 1555, during a time of famine, at Aldeburgh 'there grew Peas miraculously among the rocks, without any earth at all about them about the end of September, and brought down the price of Corne'.[30]

Although James never makes use of the word Shuck (or its Suffolk equivalent, Shock) to refer to the East Anglian bogie beast that usually appears in canine form, the subject of Tale 8, 'The Hell Hound', is clearly this entity. James describes 'a large black dog, with fiery eyes, and a fierce appearance' haunting the salt marshes near Aldeburgh. The next two tales, 'A Toad Story' and 'Charms and Cures' are really examples of local lore rather than narratives. James copied one charm from its owner, who

---

[28] Adams (1914), pp. 128–30.

[29] See Newton, M., *Savage Girls and Wild Boys: A History of Feral Children*, 2nd edn (London: Faber and Faber, 2010), pp. 50–83.

[30] Quoted in Gurdon (1893), p. 92.

claimed it had been given to her by the witch of Loddon who is the subject of Tale 1.

Tale 12, 'Bogies Ancient and Modern', begins by describing how sounds of battle were heard in the air above a seaside town after the Battle of Worcester in 1651. This seems to be a garbled version of an earlier story published in pamphlet form during the English Civil War. In August 1642 the inhabitants of Aldeburgh heard 'an uncouth noise of war' in the sky above the town, which was followed by 'melodious music'.[31] Adams plagiarised an important part of this tale, which describes a belief in the birth of webbed-footed girls with homicidal tendencies.[32] The collection of this piece of folklore, like many others, has been wrongly ascribed to Adams by several folklorists.

Influence on M. R. James?

Given his intense interest in local matters, it is hard to imagine that M. R. James did not, at some point, read his cousin's collection of East Anglian folklore. It seems reasonable to ask, therefore, whether there is any evidence that M. H. James influenced the Cambridge academic's supernatural fiction. At the time *Bogie Tales of East Anglia* was published, M. R. James had not yet embarked on his stories. His first ghost story, 'Canon Alberic's Scrap-Book', was not written until 1892. The most obvious commonality between the ghost stories of M. R. James and M. H. James's *Bogie Tales* is the significance of the Suffolk coast, which is central to two of M. R. James's best loved stories: 'Oh Whistle, and I'll Come to You, My Lad' (1904) and 'A Warning to the Curious' (1925). However, given the James family's connection with Aldeburgh, it is hardly surprising that

---

[31] Walsham, A., 'Invisible helpers: angelic intervention in post-Reformation England', *Past and Present* 208 (2010), pp. 77–130, at pp. 89–90.

[32] Adams (1914), p. 138.

the town would feature in the writings of two different members of the family.

Folklore makes an appearance in some of M. R. James's stories, most notably 'The Ash-tree' (with its theme of witchcraft) and 'A Warning to the Curious', for which M. R. James wove an entirely new legend about the buried three crowns of East Anglia. The connection between ghosts and treasure (which is also the theme of Tale 11 in *Bogie Tales*) recurs a few times in M. R. James's short stories. On the whole, however, James's stories focus not on folk tradition but on learned antiquarian studies and magic. James also displayed little interest in folklore in his popular itinerary of East Anglia, *Suffolk and Norfolk* (1930). While none of Margaret James's 'bogies' seem to resemble the ghosts and monsters of her cousin's fiction, the eccentric squires of 'Lost Hearts' (1892–3) and 'Mr Humphreys and His Inheritance' (1911) recall some of the characters from the Suffolk coast described by Margaret James. Could 'Squire Springfield' (Tale 15), the nocturnal squire who builds himself a room with ingeniously concealed doors in a Neoclassical hunting lodge, and who takes in and raises an abandoned baby, have inspired the much more sinister Mr Abney of 'Lost Hearts'? It is impossible to say with certainty.

Others may well notice connections between *Bogie Tales* and the fiction of M. R. James that I have failed to spot, and I shall be delighted if they do so. However, I find no obvious indications that, even if he read his cousin's *Bogie Tales*, M. R. James was influenced by this material. Instead, the major influence on James who included elements of folklore in his stories was the Irish writer Joseph Sheridan Le Fanu.[33] As Andrew Smith has observed, ghost story writers of the late nineteenth and early twentieth centuries revived the spectres of folklore in reaction to the anodyne, 'purposeless' ghosts that had

---

[33] Smith, A., *The Ghost Story, 1840–1920: A Cultural History* (Manchester: Manchester University Press, 2010), pp. 151–3.

become the subjects of parapsychological investigation.[34] In addition, M. R. James was contemptuous of Spiritualism, mocking it in 'The Treasure of Abbot Thomas' (1904). James drew on the resources of folklore to revive the traditional, pre-modern ghost – or something like it. James's malevolent monsters are often akin to the strange, inexplicable bogies of folklore, like 'The Hateful Thing' of *Bogie Tales*. Once again, none of this means that James was directly inspired by his cousin; but it is undeniable that both Jameses were steeped in a common East Anglian tradition of supernatural lore where some very unsettling horrors lurked.

[34] Ibid. p. 3.

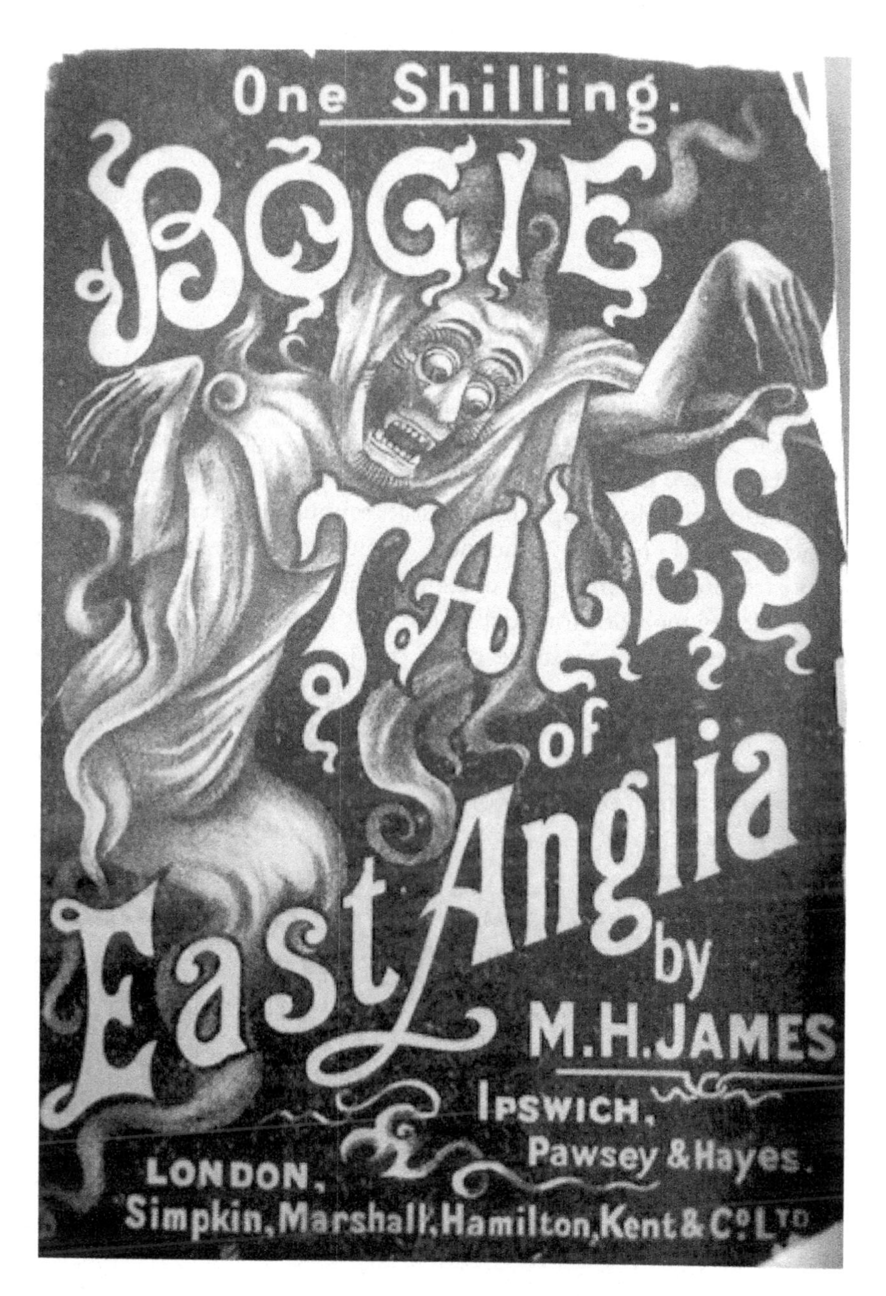

The original front cover of Bogie Tales of East Anglia (1891).

Editor's note

I have made minimal changes in this edition to the text of *Bogie Tales of East Anglia* as it appears in the 1891 edition by Pawsey & Hayes. I have rationalised M. H. James's use of single and double quotation marks, applying double quotation marks only to speech, and I have amended some eccentric uses of the apostrophe. The principal change is the addition of numbers to the tales, which do not exist in the first edition, and the addition of my own notes to those of M. H. James (which appeared as endnotes in the first edition, and here feature as footnotes). All notes are mine unless identified by the letters [MHJ] to indicate that the note was authored by M. H. James herself. Any errors in the transcription or editing of the text are mine.

Preface to the 1891 edition

Many of these Stories were told the writer as a child, and many others she collected with some little difficulty, in later years – others were collected by a friend, who kindly entrusted her with the results of his inquiries, and who was fortunate in striking a hitherto unworked vein of folk-lore, as regards the district in which he lived.

Whilst three of the stories are in print, none of the others have, as yet, it is believed, been published, or even taken down in writing; and most of them were gathered from the lips of entirely illiterate people, who for a long while had no suspicion that what they told was to be published.

The moment this idea entered their minds they became silent know-naughts, or else deliberately refused to tell any more tales, though previously they had revelled in finding an attentive listener.

"That's all a pack o' nonsense," they would say, "You don't want to hear all that rubbish; you don't believe a word of it," although one knew they had numbers of tales to tell, in the truth of which they implicitly believed.

Others frankly said, "It was not lucky to print such tales; 'they' did not like to have it done," The unexplained and mysterious 'they,' referring to the bogies!

The collection is not presented as being in any sense exhaustive, and, indeed, only touches the fringe of what is, doubtless, a very mine of folk-lore, as nearly all the Stories were told along the Suffolk coast, and beside the river Waveney.

M. H. J.

Introduction to the 1891 edition

In both the Eastern counties the fighting spirit has always been strong, from the days of Boadicea, till the present time, and in the earlier ages the coast was frequently ravaged by the Danes and other Northern pirate warriors. Many of these invaders were buried in mounds, or tumuli, which are found in every part, almost, of East Anglia; and in these mounds curious treasures have occasionally been found of armour, drinking vessels, and rings. These 'finds' have justified the legends of hidden treasure, presided over by animal spirits.

The battles have, no doubt, peopled the district with 'ghosties,' as they are called, whilst the wild marsh land, intersected with dykes, as in Holland, into which the sea sometimes breaks irresistibly, and over which the will-o'-the-wisp is seen to flitter, are weird enough to give rise to endless superstitions.

A seafaring life, too, is known to deepen the belief in the supernatural, and it is usual for all the lads, in most of the places mentioned, to 'make the voyages' before settling down to work 'on the land.' This means to go for a few years to the deepest cod-fishing off the distant banks.

When it is remembered that unwritten tradition survives quite marvellously, until people learn to read; and that the terror caused by 'bogies' must have been valuable to the smugglers, who honeycombed the two counties, as scares to keep inquisitive folk from their hiding places, it is, I think, in some measure explained how those stories have been preserved in all their freshness, and how the spirit is maintained amongst the people which will actually develop fresh supernatural beliefs in this prosaic century.

In my investigations of the legends belonging to the villages between Beccles and Bungay, on the Norfolk side of the River Waveney, I was so fortunate as to strike an almost undiscovered lode in the rich mines of folk-lore, for which East Anglia is famous.

Legends of the fen-folk, of clapping-gates, of the hell beast, or the churchyard animal, of the interchangeability of human and animal forms, and many others, were the rewards of a somewhat laborious search, whilst I also collected a few charms and cures, which are still in daily use among the country folk.

And here, let me say, that though 'silly Suffolk' has passed into a proverb and a reproach, not justified by the derivation of the word ('selig,' German – blessed and happy), and though Norfolk, from its contiguity, shares the character, it is a great mistake to set down the East Anglians as a stupid race. They are slow, but extremely shrewd, and in conversation amongst themselves you may hear passages of the finest dry wit, while their deductions are very closely drawn from the constant and keen observation of natural objects. In common with the Swiss, they suffer from home-sickness, and are deeply attached, even in these wandering days, to their original homes. The men and women, who make use of the charms I am about the recount, are not fools, though they may be foolish.

BOGIE TALES OF EAST ANGLIA

"I cannot tell how the truth may be,
I tell the tale as 'twas told to me."

1

Lucky Chance.[35]

Her name wasn't rightly Chegriff (Chergrave), nor yet Mary, but we called her "Mary Chegriff."[36] She was not born at Loddon, but her mother brought her back from a journey. Yes, the witch made long journeys, sometimes for two years at a time. The witch's girl was named Mara,[37] or Mora, something like Maria.

"Mrs. Crab got the child baptized. She was a good Bible woman."

"The witch was proper and spiteful, and said the child was bound over to Satan, and it was only cruelty to make her go agin him."

"Mary wasn't a witch. She was a real, proper nice girl. Once when she was at school she did larn some little ones to read by the charm. I don't rightly remember the charm, but there was brain-wort, and red-wort, and gold-wort, and silver-wort in it. The parson, he went after her mother, but the wise woman had never spoken to the child, and then they found that Mary

---

[35] Collected from entirely illiterate persons, and given in the vernacular [MHJ].

[36] Chedgrave is the next village to Loddon, on the opposite side of the River Chet.

[37] *Mara*, name akin with 'night-mare,' the incubus of Northern mythology [MHJ].

learned charms by morning dreams. The parson told her she'd go to hell, sure enough, if she dreamed any more such dreams, so she left off, (fancy dreaming at will!) and she got the Bible prize at the school. The witch said, 'What's the good, Satan ain't going to give up the child; and I tell you, she's bound over!'"

"The parson let Mary go to Communion, and after that she could not sleep in her mother's house, because she used to spoil the herb tea that the witch used to send East; so Mary went to sleep along Mrs. Crab's, together."

"The old witch was a fair woman, browned; O! she was something rich, and she was clever, too; she could read foot-lines, and hand-lines, and stars – and she was always right. 'Gold or nothing,' she used to say, and so people paid her well. She was always after herbs."

"She had two rare noted imps; she could make 'em tell her what she chose, they was a male and a female."

"Impses is right little sort of fairy, like a person, right enough, but with wings like a bat. These imps could get any size they liked, but they kept as small as a bat, mostly. The witch let them bite women who wanted to become witches, and she kept 'em in an old thick box."

"The witch was never cruel to Mary. No, she never let her work, and she gave her rare nice clothes, but after she got confirmed the old witch beat her sometimes, so the girl stayed over to Mrs. Crab's."

"Heart alive, she was pretty. Never heard of Chegriff Mary? Why, all the gentry used to say she was the prettiest girl they'd seen! She was right tall, and just a little pretty colour, rather thin and white, and a lot of pretty hair, golden or brown."

"Wonderful healthy she was, and rare loving, and always did needlework for any as asked her. The girls used to be powerful spiteful at her, but she was rare toward."[38]

---

[38] *Toward* – friendly; here, the opposite of *froward* [MHJ].

"She never was one for the men; she was rather stammed[39] and shy, and very touchy if the men spoke to her; she wasn't afraid of her mother, but she used to get skeary;[40] and she had a bit of mountain ash, and a bit of a horseshoe, and a Bible, that Mrs. Crab made her carry in her pocket; she never wore a bright colour, but she wore rare good stuff; she made her own dress, mostly."

"When her mother took her to bed, she stayed with her for days; she was right good to her."

"There was nothing the matter with the witch; she just laid up comfortable, because her time was nigh up;[41] and Mary used to stay with her always, though Chance, the pedlar, played his fiddle outside."

"He was a man came about Loddon for about a year. Chance wasn't his name, but everybody called him 'Chance' – the girls called him 'Lucky Chance.' He had rare nice things in his pack, and he used to let the girls buy them for kisses, and some of the old women too!"

"How did he get his money? 'O! he had a little old fiddle, and anybody'd give all their money to hear him play.'"

"What was he like? 'O! he said he was Danish, or something foreign – a rare nice looking chap, with a right short yellow beard; he used to wear a fisherman's jersey, and a fur cap, and big boots; his hair wasn't like a foreigner, but cut right short; he used to play his little old fiddle in Loddon 'public' and fill the house, and we girls used to listen at the window. Everybody said Chance came from foreign parts to find Mary, and when he was come she used to laugh at him, but he used to make everybody laugh or cry, just as he chose. The Chegriff witch gave him a rare

---

[39] 'Stam': 'to astonish; to overcome with amazement' (Forby, R., *The Vocabulary of East Anglia* (J. B. Nichols and Son: London, 1830), vol. 2, p. 323).

[40] 'Skeary': scared.

[41] This witch only died about twenty years ago [MHJ].

ducking with hot water when he came to ask if Mary would like a little music."

"Mary didn't keep company with him – No; she only spoke to him now and again, over a hedge."

"I mind when the witch died; it was harvest-home night, and there was a rare supper in the biggest barn near Loddon – all the men off three farms, and women and girls as well. Chance had climbed on to the biggest beam, and sat there playing his fiddle, with a beer jug by him, and the men chucked him up bread and meat."

"All of a sudden, in walked Mary Chegriff. 'O, mother is dying,' she said, 'will Mrs. Crab come with me?' Well, all the women pretty nearly went, but when we got to the witch's cottage some of us daren't go upstairs, but Mary and Mrs. Crab and I (my informant), and another girl, went into the witch's bedroom. O, dear, we were frightened, the old witch had on a scarlet and brown dress, like a man's, almost, and she stood in the middle of the room. Then she began to curse! I ran to the window and hollered, 'Chance! Lucky Chance!' and there he stood, as white as a ghost! The witch said, 'Mara, take these imps, and let them bite your breasts, and you'll be a greater witch than I have been. Don't you let the devil be your master, but make him mind you.'"

"The imps were in a carved wood box; there were lots of funny things in the room, and a lot of gold on the counterpane."

"'You are never to marry, Mara,' said the witch. 'You needn't look like that; I done you a good turn when I bound you to Satan, and he's bound to have you.' And then the old witch had an awful fit, and died shrieking. We all went downstairs, except Mary, and we heard an imp call to be let out of the box. There were about twenty women in the kitchen, and a great fire – and we lit lots of candle."

"In about an hour Mrs. Crab went upstairs, and found Mary had covered up her mother with a sheet, and was crying and praying."

"Then Mary came downstairs, and she carried the box of imps, and one imp cried like a child; the box was sealed; rare funny."

"Then the women said, 'Are you going to be a witch, Mary?' 'No,' said she; 'I'll burn these.' Then the women said, 'Look, first, we have none on us ever seen an imp; open the box,' and Mary stood right still, and looked rare curious (peculiar, not inquisitive). I believe she would have opened it, because it was in her blood, you know, and one imp laughed; just then Lucky Chance played something said outside, and Mary put the box on the fire, and the imps howled, and we all went out of the cottage."

"They wouldn't bury the witch at Loddon, so Mary took the body to Norwich."

"Lucky Chance married Mary, with a special license that cost fifty pounds.[42] Mrs. Crab says that Lucky told her he would take Mary to the East; but that might have been only his fun."

"Lots of people say that the pedlar was the devil, and that he got Mara after all; but Mrs. Crab said, 'Chance was God's angel, and Mary had been bounden to the devil, but Satan'll have to do with his bounden rights over her.'"

"I saw them go off, on to a ship (said my informant) at Yarmouth; and Mary kissed him, I believe that was the first time she did it."

"We never heard of them again. Poor Mary!"

---

[42] A marriage licence from the archbishop of Canterbury would allow a couple to get married without banns or somewhere other than the parish church.

2

The Hateful Thing.

There is an uncomfortable sort of ghostly terror, in beast form, that haunts villages on the borders of the two counties, which is commonly called the 'Hateful Thing.'[43] I allude to the churchyard or hell-beast. This charming creature generally takes the somewhat indefinite form of a 'swoundling:' i.e., swooning shadow, whatever that may be![44] Whenever it is met in any locality, it is a sign that some great and unusually horrible wickedness is about to be committed, or has just taken place there.

---

[43] *The Hateful Thing* is said to be quite Greek in character, as it is its very undefinable nature that constitutes its terror. It also partakes of the character of the Church beast, which was driven over the threshold of every new Church by the devout Norse colonizers here, as in their own land, in order that the Devil, who claimed the first living thing that entered a church, might be satisfactorily compounded with. The beast was then walled up in the building, and was supposed to issue forth on nights of omen, or before great events, and to hobble through the township, stopping and howling after its kind before the house where Death stood on the threshold. (See 'Godfather's Picture Book,' by Hans Christian Andersen.) [MHJ] (nothing in the story James mentions seems to resemble anything in this tale).

[44] Adams (1914), p. 188 gives the meaning of 'swounding' as 'something that would produce a swoon'. See Forby (1830), vol. 2, p. 337.

The writer, when crossing a field at night, once came on a countryman who had just seen this apparition, but a slight search for the goblin was wholly unsuccessful.

One carefully authenticated story, from a host of others on the same subject, may prove interesting; it is given in the words of the narrator, a respectable old charwoman, who appears wholly unimaginative, and who is the mother of a large family.

Mrs. S. tells her story as follows: "My youngest daughter, A., was keeping company with a young man; they hadn't got as far as 'arming it,' let alone 'waisting it' yet (these terms of country courtship explain themselves). So A. she says to me, 'Mother,' she say, 'a walk in the evening'd do you good, do you come along of us.' I went along, together, as they seemed to want me, unusual daughter! and A. and the young man took me to Gillingham; and then, about eight or nine, we came back to Geldeston, over market path, and it was that time I saw the Hateful Thing. Just as we got over the stile, into the road, A. say, 'Mother,' she says, 'how that dog did frighten me!' I says, 'Where?' And neither me, nor the young man see any dog."

"'It's on ahead,' says A., 'and, O, it ain't a dog, it's bigger than a horse now, and it's walking slow.' Now, I began to get skeary, and I minded that A. had been born under the chime hours (i.e., eight, twelve, and four at night), so she could see things."

"Well, A. clung to her young man, and I listened, and I heard a thumping, but I could see nothing. 'Well,' A. said, 'O, we are just agin it,' and the young man struck with his stick about the road. Then A., she come over and cling hold of me – and *the moment she touched me I saw* the Hateful Thing. The beast was black, and didn't keep the same size, and it wasn't any regular shape. We walked slow, for I was afraid of it's getting behind us, and we kept just agin it. I *lost sight of it every time A. left hold of me.* The young man wasn't a bit afraid, he saw nothing, but he heard the thumping. Well, we went on half-a-mile, and it was terrible passing Gelders, for I had seen things there afore. (Gelders is a clump of trees by the roadside, where, traditions says, there lay a stone on which the Danne gelt[45] was paid)."

"The beast kept on afore us, till it came to the sandy lane that go up to the churchyard, and went off there; and we went up the village, and A.'s young man had to go right back up the road, for he came from Beccles."

The seeing by contact is the curious feature of this tale, which the woman and her daughter fully believe.

---

[45] Danegeld: tribute paid to the Danish invaders by England's Anglo-Saxon population.

3

Ghosts on Wheels.

In this particular village, where the latest manifestation of the Hateful Thing took place,[46] there are about three hundred inhabitants, who still treasure amongst themselves a number of strange superstitions and ghost stories.

One of these is common to a good many districts, though here it has one or two modifications, which mark it as fully indigenous to the neighbourhood, at least in this form. There is a hill sloping up from the road to the churchyard and glebe waste, separated from it and the fields by a narrow, sandy lane. This hill is called Bigod's Hill, from the family name of the old Earls of Norfolk, who were always turbulent nobles;[47] one, indeed, having defied the King of those times about a trifling

---

[46] Geldeston, Norfolk.

[47] *Bigods.* From this family the present well-known Captain Boycott is descended [MHJ]. A reference to the land agent Charles Cunningham Boycott (1832–97), whose ostracisation when he was working in Ireland gave the English language the word 'boycott'. At the time of publication of *Bogie Tales*, Boycott was working for the Adair family at Flixton Hall, Suffolk. See Norgate, G. Le G. (rev. A. P. Baker), 'Boycott [*formerly* Boycatt], Charles Cunningham', *Oxford Dictionary of National Biography*, online edition, doi.org/10.1093/ref:odnb/3100, accessed 15 February 2019.

matter of taxes, and led him a long chase across country to his castle at Bungay, as is described in a well-known fragmentary ballad.[48] The last of this family, in a direct line, seem to have been utterly irreligious and profane persons, though I have never heard in what precise way they gained such a reputation.[49] Therefore, for their sins, they can never rest in their graves, but, nightly, in a huge old leathern coach, with four fiery horses, do their unshrived[50] ghosts drive abroad, along the high road (from Bungay), that passes the church, down the lover's lane – that Foster[51] might delight to draw – down the other sandy lane that skirts the grounds of Bigod's hill, and home – home, *where*? along the low road.

Now, this coach ghost is, as I have said, common to many places. It particularly belongs to the park of an Irish gentleman, but there it is never heard except as a death portent, and generally the sound is as of many coaches driving up to and leaving the front of the house.

The restless Bigods do not bring summons of death, nor do they drive up to houses; they keep always to their one round, as regularly as any old ladies in the park. They do not always rest content with one drive in the twenty-four hours, but have been encountered on the upper road. The peculiarity of the case is this, no one has ever at one and the same time both *heard* and *seen* the phantom coach. It is much more often heard than seen; and I have been told by a person of education, whom I should not credit with much imagination, that when resting on the hedge, the sound of the coach driving furiously towards her was so vivid, that, with no recollection whatever of the legend, she rose

---

[48] See Suckling, A., *The History and Antiquities of the County of Suffolk* (John Weale: London, 1846), vol. 1, pp. 134–6.

[49] The last Bigod was Roger Bigod (c. 1245–1306), 5th earl of Norfolk.

[50] Unshriven: individuals who did not make their confession or receive the last rites before death.

[51] The landscape artist Myles Birket Foster (1825–99).

and walked a little way along the road to see what was coming, when the sound drew nearer and nearer, and, finally, reached and passed her as she stood, and then she remembered and knew it was the wicked Bigods. Those who have seen the coach are few and of the last generation (though not yet old), and their descriptions given after many years are not, perhaps, worth recording.

One thing, the sceptic acquainted with the Bigods' route will, at least, admire, and that is the marvellous skill of their driver, who pilots his ponderous vehicle and fiery steeds down such narrow, and sandy, and rutty ways, with never a 'spill.'

Poor creatures! theirs is a harder fate than that of the Wandering Jew[52] – *they* get no change of scene.

At Spixworth, in Norfolk, is an old country house with a well-known ghost attached, of which the following stories are told: – "The place was let a Captain and Mrs. B., who had not long been in residence when, one evening, as they were starting for a dinner party, on their way down the drive, the lady said to her husband, 'Oh! do look at that hearse! What can it be doing here?' And at the same moment the horses swerved violently. The husband peering out, saw nothing, and said so; but the lady persisted that she had seen a hearse. At dinner that night the gentleman who took her to table, after asking how Mrs. B. liked the house, said, 'Oh! by the bye, I suppose you haven't seen the Spixworth ghost yet?' 'No,' she answered, 'I did not know that we lived in a haunted house: what is the ghost?' 'Oh! really, have you never heard of the *Spixworth hearse*?' he asked. Heard of it! – why she had but just *seen* it! Neither Captain nor Mrs. B. had any superstitious fears, but they were, in point of fact, driven from Spixworth by the extraordinary noises which were heard in the house, which so alarmed the servants that they could not keep any. At twelve at night, so the servants said, these loud and

---

[52] The legend of a Jew who taunted Jesus at his crucifixion and was then condemned to wander the earth for eternity.

dreadful noises began, and such knocking at their doors, as banished sleep. Captain and Mrs. B. decided to be in the servants' quarter, together, at the time when these disturbances took place, and found there had been no exaggeration. At twelve the hubbub began, and knocks, loud and angry, fell thick on the door by which they themselves were standing, and though they had a light they could discover no sort of cause."

At the present time the owners of the house are living there themselves, and I am not informed whether they are disturbed in like manner, or whether it was only outsiders who were so troubled.

4

Goblin Ground.

I suppose – to return to the Geldestone Bogies – that lovers are inordinately bold persons, or that they are so self-absorbed as to take no heed of what would alarm ordinary mortals. At all events, the lover's walk just skirts the glebe and churchyard, is completely arched over by trees, and is reached by a haunted lane or road, whichever way you enter it!

One danger is, of course, that they may encounter the Bigods on their weary round, another has been indicated in the story of the 'Hateful Thing,' but there are yet four more dangers of a supernatural kind, which, unless one is in love and well supported (or engaged in 'mothing,'[53] as in my own case), would certainly take the edge off one's desire to walk there.

The short way to the next village crosses the park by a grass path, and the glebe field by a footpath, ending in some steps down the roots of a tree, and just skirting a large horse pond, which, in rainy weather, is sometimes too full to admit of people getting by, so that they needs must go along 'Hodman's path'[54] at the bottom of the field, to the gate. After one of these

---

[53] Presumably searching for specimens of moths.

[54] *Hodman's Path.* The narrow green strip at the inner foot of a field hedge, just wide enough for a snail or 'dodman' to pass along [MHJ].

overflows, it was determined to deepen the pond, and whilst this was in progress the workmen came upon a skeleton in the mud at the bottom of the pond, round whose neck was chained a large piece of millstone, whereupon they began to recollect old stories told them by their grannies, of a wicked felon who, for his sins, was condemned to be buried at the 'four-releet,' or four cross ways, but from respect to his family was after all deposited in the pond, where he had lain undisturbed ever since.

The churchyard of the village was a long way off, so it was arranged by consent of the then Rector of Geldestone that the skeleton should be freed from its millstone and laid close to the wall on the north side of the churchyard, which was only across the park and fields.

Never was a more rash deed than the loosening of the millstone – Ingratitude seems bound up in the bones of a ghost (when he has any) – and this wicked felon, relieved of his spiritual clog, rose at once from his dry and uncomfortable churchyard quarters, and, nightly, with a horrid clanking of ghostly chains, rambles about the unconsecrated space of glebe between the churchyard and Lovers' Lane.

The millstone had been wisely put round his graceless neck to prevent his walking, and now it was gone he up and walked; ay! and does so still. So much for being wiser than the ancients!

One would think the 'Hateful Thing' would resent any other animal sharing his Bogie-dom, but whether he do so or no, certain it is that, on the very spot where the felon and the 'Hateful' ramble at night, another creature joins the party. This is said to be a donkey, with chains. Pooh-poohed, of course, by all wise people, who said, the glebe being let for pasture, no doubt the chains were those of the donkey hobbled there; and the unwise strove to believe them. But wise and unwise were alike confounded when it was discovered that, granted, there was a fleshly ass tethered on the glebe, and granted he did rattle his chains, *there was another beast* – another donkey that rattled his.

"Echo," said a wise one, but he was withered with scorn. "Echoes! there ain't none in miles" (and there is not).

When to this cheerful trio in the glebe is added a white figure, probably that before mentioned as a form of the 'Hateful': i.e., the swounding shadow, which walks the green at the mouth of the lane, and did there scare an M.A. of Oxford, his sister, and two friends; and a ghost which deserves fuller description once seen in the green lane leading to the village, it must surely be confessed that the lovers of Geldestone have need of stout heart and clear consciences if they would walk at evening in the Lover's Lane. "Gamekeeper in moonlight" was suggested for the M.A.'s ghost. "There was *no* moonlight," was the crushing answer. "Maltster in white slop,[55] poaching," was put forward. "Maltsters *walk*, I believe? and this figure *glided*."

Everyone knows a ghost when he sees one – and this was a ghost – we hunted for it, and there was nothing, not even footprints on the heavy dew, "and a man must have touched the ground," answered my informant, not, I need hardly say, the M.A.

---

[55] 'Slop': 'An outside garment, reaching to mid-leg, worn by children, and by some workmen' (Forby (1830), vol. 2, p. 307).

5

A Wraith.

The last bogie was seen only by two persons, one the chief washerwoman of the village, a woman, the wife of a long service soldier, who was born near London, and had since been to India and far a-field – the other her little girl.

She had been to take the washing home to the Hall with her little girl to help, and was rather anxious too, because once before the cattle had charged her and frightened her a good deal, so that she arrived across the lawns in front of the house running with all her might and carrying her big baskets – and another time the little dog had flown at her ankles.

"So I felt a bit timid-like," she said. "Well, I got the things safe to the Hall, and Hetty and me, we set off home along o' the barrow with the baskets in. Well, you know, Miss, what they call Kell's Heath, we came along that way, and we was turning into the green lane to come down by Master John Hobbe's house (this lane was in a straight line with another, which led to Lovers' Lane) – when running along in front of me I see a young woman, that hadn't been behaving nice to me of late. She was walking at first, but as soon's I see her, she set on running. Why, Miss M——, I see her as plain as I see you now, that's the truth, though my husband he do laugh at me when I say so. Well, I says to Hetty: 'Hetty,' I says, 'there's So-and-So' (I won't name the young woman, Miss, though she'd no call to behave as she done to me). 'Where, mother?' says Hetty, and then she saw her too – and I says, 'put down the barrow child and stay you there while I go after her.' That was pretty dark in the lane, but I give you my word, Miss M—— we wasn't a bit frightened, not a bit – or I should never a left Hetty, but that never came into my head but 'twas the girl herself – and I thought, 'well *I* don't bear no malice against her, so I'll catch her up and tell her she didn't ought to 'ave acted so, but that's all bye-gones.' Seemingly when she see me coming, she fare 'shamed to meet me, she run up o'the hedge and through the brambles into the field that go down to the low road. I run up the hedge too a-calling of her, but then – I couldn't see none of her, so I was fair and scared, and I called out to Hetty to bring the barrow along, and we looked up and down, and, since the dew fell, if you'll believe me, Miss, there'd been none there but us, not a footmark of any one, nor a bit of a gap in the hedge. Well, I was that frightened I hardly knew how to get home – but Hetty she helped with the barrow, and we did get home at last; I was all of a tremble, but my husband he give me a drop of brandy to calm me down like, but he 'on't hear on it that I see anything, but indeed I did, Miss M——, I see her as plain as I see you this minute – and I ha'int been well since."

The next day the poor washerwoman was stricken by a bad attack of heat apoplexy, from which she has never fully recovered – and she lays her illness in a great measure to the fright she had that night. Though it is quite possible that her various frights in going to the Park in the heat had predisposed her to hallucinations, and that her illness was then coming on. Nothing was ever heard of the young woman's doings that night, except that she was not anywhere near the place – her home was somewhere Alderton way, I believe – and I daresay she never heard of her own wraith.

There was another bogie down near Master John's – in a large comfortable old house, but no one would tell the story to us, possibly because one of the collectors was living there. A housemaid left because of the frights she said she had constantly in my bedroom – she had thought the place very dull and intended to leave, but then decided to stay, till after these scares; which, till I knew we were joint tenants with a bogie, I believed to be due to a white dress hanging in the door in the moonlight.

6

A Were-dog Story.

This tale,[56] which runs as follows, is still common talk among the beachmen at Lowestoft. An Italian gentleman, with curly hair and a very dark complexion, asked a fisher-boy, of Lowestoft, to become his page, but this the boy refused, as he did not wish to go to foreign parts; whereupon the Italian, far from being angry, asked the boy to look after a dog for him, as he was going away.

Now, the dog had been seen in the town, and its ownership was well known, though, strange to say, the dog and his master had never been seen together. It was a fine dog, a large, curly black retriever, very long and lean.

When the fisher-boy found the gentleman had really gone away, he began to look after the dog, for which he had been very handsomely paid beforehand. Every morning the boy, who was

---

[56] *Were-Dog and Loup-garou.* A very general Mediaeval and even classical superstition was that of lycanthropy, or the power possessed by human beings of changing at will into savage beasts. It is even found amongst the Hottentots; but, I believe, there are not many traces of the belief in England proper, though I have seen the idea in a recent ballad, in Scotch form, by a well-known poetess – and it occurs in 'Hugues le Loup,' by M. M. Erckmann-Chatrian [MHJ]. The reference is to Erckmann-Chatrian, M. M., *Hugues-le-Loup: Contes de la Montagne* (Paris: Levy, 1860).

fourteen years old, went out to swim in the sea, and the dog went with him.

One day, when the boy had swum further than usual, he found that the dog savagely resented his returning to shore, with such growlings and menaces, that the terrified boy was obliged to swim on and on, still further out to sea, whilst the dog swam close behind him.

At last, the boy turning his head round in desperation, saw, to his intense and almost benumbing terror, the dark, saturnine face of the Italian gentleman *close beside him* – the metamorphosis was only momentary, and on looking round again he saw the dog had reappeared, and by continued and fierce growling and biting still urged him out to sea.

Fortunately a smack, under press of sail, scudded by, and the boy was able to attract the notice of those on board, who came to his rescue, but his neck and shoulder were bleeding from the dog's angry attack. The animal was seen to dive like a porpoise, and, re-appearing a great distance off, swam away. The boy's name was M—— and he used to work, in slack times, at a tanyard in the lower part of the old town of Lowestoft, so 'tis said.

After the remarkable escape above recorded, it was remembered, on all sides, how many boys of about fourteen years old were yearly drowned off the town, and how, in particular, only a year or so back a boy's body had been found washed up off Ness Point, with the marks of a dog's teeth on the neck and shoulder, which till now had been placed to the credit of an attempt to save life on the part of some noble animal.

7

The Wild Boy.

In a small seaside place in Suffolk,[57] with which I am well acquainted, there still thrive a good many queer and eerie stories of byegone days, and some of the very present.[58]

The town lies along a shore, with a river to the south, and the salt marshes to the north, water on three sides, and the barrenest marsh lands all around. In these marshes, some seven miles south of the town, about a hundred years ago, some fishermen, returning from the sea, beheld a strange creature disporting itself, sometimes on the grass, sometimes in the water; they gazed astonished, for the thing was like a big lad, all covered with hair of a reddish colour, but entirely naked. They took counsel together and surrounded the creature, entangling him in their nets, so that they made a prisoner of him, and in spite of all his struggles they bore him off to the Castle, where he was shown to the Governor, who was very much interested.

By his desire this strange amphibious being was left at the Castle, where he was carefully examined, and it was then found

---

[57] Orford, Suffolk.

[58] *The Wild Boy.* This story, which may be found in a very old guide-book, long since out of print, is also, sometimes, referred to King John's reign. I prefer the later version [MHJ].

that, as far as articulate speech went, he was dumb, though that he had all the proper organs could not be doubted, from the varied range of sounds he would utter; his hearing, too, was marvellously acute. He was supplied with clothes, but he never could be induced to keep them on for long at a time; and, at first, would go into the most violent rage if they were brought out. He would not speak, even after the greatest pains had been taken to teach him; and so sure were his instructors that he *could* speak if he would, that, upon his refusal, they tied him by his heels to the smoke jack, 'in hopes *that* would make him.' (Did they think the words were blocked in the poor imp's throat?) Sometimes he was allowed to go and play about in the sea, with men in a boat to watch him, or at first he was tied to a rope. These water frolics were his delight, but, as once he tried to escape, they were put a stop to.

There had been an idea of presenting him to the King, if he could but be taught a few Christian accomplishments, and as a first step he was baptized 'George,' but his violent and sullen temper proved an obstacle to all plans of improving him; and he was at length condemned to be turnspit; which duty he performed very well. He would sit for hours brooding in the corner of the settle by the fireplace, holding his great queer head in both his hairy hands as if in pain, and no wonder if that hanging by the heels was oft repeated! At last one day he was missing, and at night some fishermen came to the Castle to report that whilst shooting their nets in the sea opposite, they had seen the wild boy swimming boldly and rapidly away from the shore. They had tried to catch him, and nearly succeeded, but he dived under their nets, and throwing up his arms uttered a joyous cry and was seen no more.

At the same place, and indeed all along the coast for about twenty miles, there prevailed (not long after the days of the wild boy, I believe) a severe local dearth, when, it is confidently maintained, a certain kind of vetch bearing ordinarily the usual inedible bean, became miraculously increased in size and fit for human food, lasting in this abnormal condition the whole time of the dearth, so that the inhabitants of those villages were fed and nourished thereby. As soon as the harvest became plentiful and there was ordinary food in abundance, the vetch, which had now gained its present name of the 'Famine Pea,' dwindled down to its original size and is not much larger now-a-days than the rest of the vetches. It still grows plentifully by the coast.

8

The Hell Hound.

At the north end of the town of A—[59] lie the salt marshes, which are sometimes full, like a lake, after rains or the prevalence of certain winds, and of which there was a sunset view exhibited in London not long ago. Here a favourite walk of the inhabitants leads across a sort of common, planted with a fir grove; by one or other of two paths, one of which goes through the pine wood and emerges near the station; the other leaves the pine wood on the left, and skirts the mere, crossing the line, and leading into a sandy lane between more pine trees.

At the sea end of this waste is a 'kissing gate' – as wickets are called in those parts – and here it is quite likely that the presiding bogie will meet you, if you walk there after dark. The bogie is a large black dog,[60] with fiery eyes, and a fierce appearance. Do not, however, be afraid of him, if you keep in the path that leads across the 'line,' for all will be well, he will walk 'to heel' as a good dog should, and will only make you feel rather nervous by his odd silent trot; but if you want to go the other way he will show you what he thinks by an awful growling, he

---

[59] Almost certainly Aldeburgh, Suffolk (the only coastal town in East Anglia beginning with the letter 'a').

[60] *The Hell Hound.* See note to 'The Hateful Thing' [MHJ].

will stand in your path and shew his teeth, he will snarl till you are almost paralysed with fear; – and then he will sit down and stare at you with his eyes aflame.

Give up your plan, or it will be the worse for you, though the dog never bites or barks, but sometimes drags you by your clothes; untold horrors befall the man and woman who persists in thwarting him.

You give up the walk under the pine trees – he ceases to growl! you step again towards the other path – his eyes no longer flame – you walk boldly on – he follows 'to heel,' as before. You reach the gate at the level crossing – he sits down and watches you out of sight, and you totter on a few steps and gladly sit down in a hedge to rest your shaking limbs.

He is like the 'dog fiend' in Peel Castle, in the Isle of Man,[61] or the 'Hateful Thing', in Norfolk.

Another walk he has, some five miles off, under an avenue of elms, that arch the entrance to a little village; and here he was met one night by the father of a servant of ours, who offended him by stopping, and was treated by him with great indignity.

If one might suggest an origin for a beast so mysterious, it seems not impossible that in smuggling days (for which the coast was notorious), there really was a clever dog trained to keep people from hunting among the trees and underbush, and that the terror of him has survived, blending probably with some older legend of a church beast.

It is strange to make a terror of a fine black dog, when many of the fishermen keep dogs, and are much attached to them, the said dogs in some cases *dying!* before tax-day, and re-appearing as well as ever, after.

---

[61] A reference to Moddey Doo, the black dog spectre of Peel Castle (see Killip, M., *The Folklore of the Isle of Man* (London: Batsford, 1975), pp. 150–1).

9

A Toad Story.

A curious story was told me by a servant, which shows how utterly hopeless it is to eradicate false ideas on natural history by any school teaching. A young man and woman, lovers, had been out walking together, and as it was rather hot they sat down on a knoll at the foot of a tree to rest. By and bye, the young woman felt very uncomfortable, but she could not, at first, feel sure what caused her discomfort. Soon, however, she became aware that something was making its way up one of her legs, and through her thin stocking she felt the horrid chill of a toad. She was terribly frightened, as she knew the toad was poisonous – *poor* toads! – and was afraid it would bite her! She tried all ways to get it off, but in vain, and it now seemed to be hanging to the lower part of the back of the calf of her leg, motionless. At last the lover saw how ill she looked, and wanted to know what was the matter. She tried to put him off, one way and another, or to get him to leave her, but he was alarmed at her looks, and insisted on being told what was distressing her so terribly. At last she said, "Well, John, if I *must* tell you, I must – there's a toad on my leg, and I can't get it off. "Lass," said he, "Aren't you promised to me? Let me get it off." At last she agreed, and he found the toad, not biting her, but hanging on by suction of his great mouth, and having raised a big swelling where he sucked. It was a very painful business to get him off, and the girl's nerves were dreadfully shaken. At first, no harm came of it, but when a little while after she was over-tired with her housework, the place where the toad had hung on her leg became, what the people term, a sloughing (pronounced *sluffing*) sore, and she was ill with it for a long while.

"I don't hold with sitting down, like that," said the narrator, "I like to be on a safe seat from them loathely toads."

10

Charms and Cures.

All babies are born with blue eyes, and it is not until they are some weeks old that there is any possibility of judging what colour the iris will eventually take; so, as brown eyes are in great favour in a part where nearly everyone has pale blue, the following charms are used to ensure the child, on whom they are tried, the certain possession of brown eyes: –

"Bind hazel twigs to the back of a new-born baby, and its eyes will turn hazel;" or, in another form – "Hang the birth chamber with hazel twigs if you wish the baby's eyes to be brown."

I have often heard the village women boast of having successfully used this charm, and certainly the effect of soft brown eyes, when combined with the usual light hair of the district, is very charming.

To ensure lucky dreams, the next charm is repeated by tramps – "Kiss a sheaf of corn in the field, under harvest moonlight, sleep in the open, and your dreams will point out luck."

In Suffolk the cure for hiccough is to stoop without bending the knees, holding the breath at the same time, and make the sign of the Cross on the toe of the boot or shoe, pressing rather hard in so doing. It is supposed to be infallible – unless you are too rheumatic to perform it properly – in which case the

Norfolk cottagers can suggest several charms and cures. Those given here were all tried by one cottager, and he was satisfied with the results!

'Vipers' oil,' obtained in some rather disagreeable way, I believe, and 'Otters' oil,' were two chief remedies; a blanket of mullein leaves,[62] spread on the bed, had great virtue; but his chief faith was in a little pouch, which he wore constantly, containing the two left feet of a mole caught at sunrise, – they were a cure for rheumatic twinges on the right side. If his pains had been on the left, he would have worn the two right feet of a mole caught at sunset – reversing the charm. He also wore as an amulet a running toad, imprisoned in a very small air-tight box, and allowed to waste to death; this unpleasant charm was never to be taken from his person until he died. The running toad is the 'natterjack'; it is generally found near the sea, and may be distinguished by a yellow stripe down its back. Neither the 'hopping toad,' nor any other sort, will be of any use against rheumatism.

Horse chestnuts gathered by children (too young to have felt rheumatism), between the two Michaelmases (i.e., September 29th and October 12th), threaded with a red-hot needle that had never touched grey yarn, he had worn as a necklace – they were a good remedy, he considered.[63]

This particular district[64] is very liable to floods in the winter, and there is, in consequence, a good deal of suffering from rheumatic affections amongst the poor people; which, I suppose, accounts for the numerous ways in which they strive to get rid of it. The most complicated charm I have heard of at

---

[62] Mullein leaf (*Verbascum thapsus*) was frequently used as a herbal remedy.

[63] *Chestnuts and grey yarn.* President Cleveland was recommended chestnuts carried in the pocket, among thirty-one remedies suggested for his rheumatism [MHJ]. A reference to Grover Cleveland, President of the United States 1885–89 and 1893–97.

[64] The eastern Waveney Valley.

present in the possession of a respectable cottager, near Loddon, to whom it was given in early girlhood, in return for some trifling service rendered to the famous Witch of Chergrave (pronounced Chergriff). I give it below: –

'Church Charm.'

To gain a husband, name known or unknown,
Make your choice on a graveyard stone,
Quarter day's night if there fare a moon,
Pass through the church gate right alone;
Twist three roses crosses from graveyard bits,
Plant them straight in your finger slits,
Over the grave hold a steady hand,
And learn the way the side crosses stand.
One is yourself, and your husband one,
And the middle one need be named of none.
If they both on the middle cross have crossed,
His name you win, and a year you've lost;
For he who lies in the namesake mould
His soul has sold – or, he would have sold,
And you give a year which the dead may use,
Your last year of earth-life that you lose.

– I have tried to write down this charm exactly as I learnt it, but as it is some years since I saw the original manuscript, a few unimportant words may have been altered.

11

Treasure Ghosts.

There was a patriarchal looking old blacksmith in A—[65] at the north end, who, with his old wife, lived in a very pretty and roomy low white house in the street, which house was so pleasant that, though it did not face the sea, it was readily let as summer lodgings.

At one time it had been quite small, and the old blacksmith, then a man of about forty-five years of age, was very poor and struggling. He dreamt one night that a white figure came to his bedside and pointed with its hand to a certain part of the bedroom wall. He, however, thought nothing of it, and it passed from his mind, till again the dream recurred, and this time the ghost was very urgent, so he got up and marked the place on the wall. Still, in broad daylight, it seemed too absurd for a sensible man to believe he had seen a ghost; so, in spite of the mark on the wall, he did nothing, until a third time the ghost appeared.

Then he decided to see what it meant and what it wanted, so he broke open the wall at the place he had marked, and there, in the wall space, discovered a skeleton mouldering away, and, by its side, a bag full of money. He quietly buried the bones, and

---

[65] Once again, almost certainly Aldeburgh.

applied the money to his own use, enlarged his house, increased his business, and prospered thenceforward, till he grew very old. He did not like any allusion to be made to the ghost, because the money was properly treasure trove, and the property of the Lord of the Manor.

A treasure ghost also appeared about seventeen miles off, to a servant girl, who lived with the family at the Abbey – a very old house.[66] She dreamt again and again of a dark, foreign sailor, with earrings, who led her to a certain stair and signed her to look under it for a purse, which he described. When she told her master and mistress they laughed at her, till on the repetition of the dream, to quiet her, they had the stair lifted, when there, before their unbelieving eyes, lay a queer old purse, of a bag shape, worked in curious and fanciful knitting, full of old and rare Spanish coins. There was an idea that the maid must know how they got there, but it was eventually proved that this suspicion was groundless.

The purse is still in existence, and I myself have seen it.

[66] Perhaps Letheringham Abbey, the seat of the Naunton family, which is located about seventeen miles from Aldeburgh.

12

Bogies Ancient and Modern.

During the Civil wars, after the battle of Worcester, when such strange portents did appear in the sky, a man from the little sea coast town[67] was visiting a friend at the inland town above-mentioned.[68] He heard, and, indeed, the whole town heard, the sound of guns and of battle in the direction of his home. Quickly putting-to his horse he drove home, in expectation of an invasion, or, at least, a naval engagement in the bay; and found on his arrival all the townsfolk, most of them in abject terror, gathered in the open, whilst overhead the awful battle raged in the sky above them! They could see (as elsewhere in the case of the battle of Naseby and other great fights), the opposing armies hurtle together, and the scene was as real and vivid as if it was being enacted on the solid ground at their feet. Some terrible hours it lasted, and then passed away, leaving the people awestricken and greatly sobered, but having done no damage to life or property.[69]

---

[67] Aldeburgh.

[68] Probably Saxmundham, Suffolk, then the closest market town inland from Aldeburgh.

[69] The Air Fight. See 'Chambers' Miscellany' [MHJ]. The reference is to Chambers, R., *The Book of Days: A Miscellany of Popular Antiquities* (W. R. Chambers: London, 1862), vol. 1, p. 154.

In the inland town a tailor died, whose ghost was seen, ay, and felt, by two of his friends, before he was known by them to be either dead or in any danger of death. The ghost advanced, swinging one arm, and looking about it as the tailor's manner was – and the two friends, who were on the pavement expecting the tailor to salute them, suddenly each received a violent blow, and found themselves prone in the road, dreadfully bruised, and one of them stunned. The other, the Dissenting minister of the place, though very sore, helped his friend into a shop, whence he eventually got home.

They kept their own counsel till the Minister had sent his servant maid to ask who was dead in the town, though as yet the bell had not been passed for a death. She soon returned, saying, "Mr. —–, the tailor, had died suddenly, at such a time that day." The very moment when their encounter with him took place! which they were able to fix with accuracy.

Not far off lived a retired military man of known character and position,[70] the bells in whose house, one Sunday, set of ringing whilst most of the household were at church.[71] It was most annoying and harassing, for the servants were constantly answering the ringing of one bell or another, that had not been pulled. At last the Major determined to put a stop to the matter, and, fearing that some silly servant's trick was at the bottom of it, called all the men and maids into the hall, so that no one could be left to work any devilry, and himself examined the whole bell system of the house, not, however, finding any signs of trickery (the hypothesis of rats had been thoroughly disposed

---

[70] The philologist and folklorist Edward Moor (1771–1848) of Great Bealings, near Woodbridge (see Seccombe, T. (rev. J. B. Katz), 'Moor, Edward (1771–1848)', *Oxford Dictionary of National Biography*, online edition, doi.org/10.1093/ref:odnb/19089, accessed 18 February 2019.

[71] *The Major's Bells*. See Mary Howitt's 'History of the Supernatural' [MHJ]. The reference is to Howitt, W. [and Howitt, M.], *The History of the Supernatural in All Ages and Nations* (London: Longman, Green, Longman, Roberts & Green, 1863), vol. 2, pp. 446–9.

of earlier). Soon the bells began, sometimes one – the sitting-room and dining-room bells rang oftenest – sometimes two, then all at once.

They were no nearer a solution than before, and the ringing went on just as ever, for about three months altogether, when, without any change in the household, everything ceased as unaccountably as it had arisen.

When Major M—— published this story[72] it led to some very curious communications made to him by a clergyman, respecting noises in his Rectory, which had, as far as he could trace, been a feature of the house for generations, but I have no details of this story.[73]

There remains only one more bogie to mention. As, on a dark night, a man with his father was fishing in the river at the south of our seaside town,[74] on the mud wall above them they heard the sound of galloping, which gradually drew nearer, till, from its position, it seemed that whatever it was, was now on the soft mud laid bare by the low tide, though the noise was as if there was a hard road under the hoofs. When by their lantern they could see the creature, instead of a horse or bull as they expected, they beheld a *tall black post*, neither more nor less! sliding with no apparent means of motion over the soft mud, accompanied by this awful noise. The son wanted to shoot at it, but the father forbade him; so the post and the noise passed on, till they were lost in the dark and the distance.

I have not succeeded in gaining any facts (?) about the quite recent witch at L——.[75] Nearly every winter the gossips seem to have some new ghost story or bogie tale to discuss, and groundless as they are for the most part, it is as well to listen to

---

[72] Moor, E., *Bealings Bells: An Account of the Mysterious Ringing of Bells at Great Bealings, Suffolk, in 1834* (John Loder: Woodbridge, 1841).

[73] *The Minister's Ghost.* See Mary Howitt's 'History of the Supernatural' [MHJ].

[74] The Alde Estuary.

[75] Perhaps a reference to the witch of Loddon.

them when possible, for some of the older and simpler folk will generally try to connect it with some half-forgotten legend which is worth preserving.

One night, I remember, whilst trying in vain to get any connected tale from a man who declared that his 'horse and cart' (!) had just been scared by something queer, an old fellow suddenly struck in with the oracular remark, 'Ah! if that had chanced *last* year on the lower road, I'd a known what it was.' I then learned that every seventh year (of which 1883 was the last), a sort of goblin creature tries to lame or kill horses on this road, in order to get their ghosts for the 'impses' to ride. It tries to lure the traveller from his cart, and then frightens the animal; the form it generally takes being that of a phantom *brown paper parcel*! but it sometimes appears as a yellow dog, or an angry cat, and will actually attack a horse or donkey. Most people believe the creature to be the ghost of an idiot boy, who was killed here by a pedlar.

On one occasion, walking back from B——[76] by night with a large party of friends, some us were astonished, in passing some trees in the hedge – elms, I think, they were – to feel a sudden glow of warmth, as if there were a fire near. We were so surprised at it, and so sure of the sensation, that we went back and passed the trees again, when again we felt the glow. It was very dark, and I thought there might be a heated haystack, of which it would be kind to tell the owner, but we found there was none at all near, and what caused the sudden heat we have never yet been able to discover.

To this region belongs a queer superstition about a race of amphibious people, with curious web feet, called the fen folk.[77] The original race was subjected to great persecution, and

---

[76] Perhaps Blythburgh, Suffolk.

[77] *Fen folk.* Lincolnshire people are often called 'yellow-bellies', i.e. frogs, other counties, as it is believed that cold-blooded, web-footed children are occasionally born in the fen districts [MHJ].

eventually died out, but not until after some few had inter-married with human beings possessed of souls.

Every now and then a web-footed child is born, generally a girl, who is a witch or fairy, with a homicidal mania – she generally drowns her victims. These creatures are always beautiful, and, unless their bare feet are seen, cannot be told from ordinary people. They are found of coming out at night to the marshes, where they commune with their own people, who live in alder bushes.

To these marshy districts is peculiar a belief that if any animal or man is impaled on a whitethorn stake the spirit is bound to haunt the spot, and, indeed, to keep within a very circumscribed area. These restless ghosts fidget uneasily, and the clapping gates are generally caused in this way, the best known of which is the famous clapping-gate of Aldeby, in Suffolk, which swings and clickets continually.

13

A Seaside Bogiedom.

There is one small seaside place along the coast[78] where nearly all the people are of kin to each other, and possess not more than four of five surnames amongst them.

They are, in spite of an extraordinary amount of inter-marrying, a fine set of people, and the men are well known for bravery in saving life at shipwrecks, and for general daring; yet they are curiously superstitious and emotional, and have a rooted dread of corpse candles, which are often seen along the sand dunes skirting the shore. They believe that these betoken the death of him who sees them, or, at the very least, some serious misfortune to his family or himself; and so much does the terror undermine their nerve that instances are not wanting in which their very belief has become a Kismet,[79] and has justified their unreasoning conviction.

The sea, too, warring ceaselessly with the land at one part of the coast, encroaches yearly, devouring shore and sand-cliff; at another, slowly receding, casts up sandy spits and alters the configuration of the shores.

---

[78] Aldeburgh.

[79] 'Kismet': fate or destiny.

In older days these encroachments were more sudden, and once the greater part of a little town was thus swept away, its streets and one of its churches submerged.

Fishermen will tell you that on still nights, when they lie out in their boats, in the bay, after the fat 'longshore herring,' the bells of the old church chime clear and sweet below the ripples, and one who had a fine imagination is said to claim to have seen, one very low tide, the walls of houses and buildings!

In the little town now in my mind there is, in spite of its prosaic exorbitance in the summer, and its almost sordid poverty in the winter, a leaven remaining of romance, which helps to preserve, in the men and women of the older generation at least, the memory of the old traditions of men and bogies familiar since their childhood.

Two novelists and three poets – nay, more – have loved that little place, which, without being beautiful, has some subtle charm, which, when once felt, draws visitors to it again and again, regardless of the attractions of other more lovely spots, though no one have I ever found able to explain the reason.

This little seaside townlet is full of odd characters and romantic histories of ghostly visitants, and not so long ago was noted for the beauty and comeliness of its women and men.

More than once or twice has the ballad of King Cophetua[80] been re-enacted there, and tragedy as well as romance has seemed, in a sort, to haunt the place, though the following fragments are of a light character.

There is a large and picturesque pond on the west road, out into the country, where once some carters, going home, found their teams at first unwilling to pass, and then absolutely determined not to go nearer. The men usually watered the horses there, and it was much frequented. This particular evening there was nothing to be seen that was in the least unusual, but so it

---

[80] A king who proverbially fell in love at first sight and proposed marriage there and then.

befel, that the stout and gentle beasts were cowering in terror and covered with foam, at the unseen object of their fear, and neither coaxing nor blows could urge them past. So the carters had to go back, and make a circuit of certainly three miles before they could get home that evening. "And none of us knows to this day *what* them horses see – nor yet what they may 'a saved us from," said one of the men.

There is in, also, the little town, a pretty lane, with a sweet-briar hedge, called after the wife of Bertrand de Guesclin,[81] haunted vaguely by a figure in white, but there is an uninteresting indefiniteness and want of detail about it which are provoking.

Coming down the slope which ends the terrace you pass along the main street of the town, hardly above the sea level. Half-way along is the chief bakery, where is sold, on New Year's Eve, a kind of cake or curiously shaped bun, called 'kitchel.'[82] There is supposed to be a special advantage in eating them on that night, and indeed they are not to be had on any other. Great ill-luck was foretold for those who did not order at least one, for each member of their household.

The cakes are about eight inches long, rather flat, and, perhaps at the widest three and a half inches, quite narrow at each end, marked in bars, and sprinkled with a few currants. I do not remember anything the least distinctive in their taste. No one has been able to tell me their origin, nor the meaning of the custom, which, as yet, I have found nowhere else, and which will probably die out on the death of the present proprietor.

Just below the churchyard, on the slope of the hill, stands a large old house,[83] possessed of two tame domestic ghosts,

---

[81] Bertrand du Guesclin (c. 1320–80), a Breton noble and Constable of France during the Hundred Years War.

[82] 'Kitchel': given as 'kickel' in Forby (1830), vol. 2, p. 180: 'a sort of flat cake with sugar and currants strewn on the top'. Jobson, A., *Under a Suffolk Sky* (London: Robert Hale, 1964), p. 92 refers to 'Kitchel Cakes at Aldeburgh, which were baked on New Year's Eve, and had to be eaten before midnight'.

[83] Possibly Wyndham House, Aldeburgh.

which have no particular history; but one is said to pass through a small bedroom in the form of a dog without a head. (Yet another ghostly dog!) The other must be like the nation that is 'happy because its annals were dull.' One of its ways was to drip very slowly, like rain through a leak, when rain there was none, nor leak either; or to sound like a solemn footstep – pit! *pat!* pit! three steps forward, and *pat!* pit! *pat!* three steps back, on an upper landing.

Another curious thing in that house was that a certain door – the door of a small square dressing-room – could never be kept shut. The room within was used as a sitting-room, and children and grown-up persons alike can testify how, as they sat in the inner room, the handle of the outer door would yield with a click, and a little draught would betray, that, as usual, the outer door had opened; and one child keenly remembers the terror of evenings spent there alone, hearing the door firmly shut by her parents going down to dine, click open in about a quarter of an hour, and *no one enter*. This door was examined by the gentleman whose room it closed, its lock was seen to, it was rehung on its hinges, battens and indiarubber were fixed – it still opened. His wife would watch to try and discover *why* it happened, but quite in vain, and it was uncured when they left the house.

Up and down the church hill, outside this house, a tall white figure wanders nightly. I have seen, what I believe is mistaken for her, myself. The white lady, as they call her, is decidedly alarming, and it is found to require some pot-valiancy to pass her at night. One old toper swore he defied her, and went home by the church hill, but some comrade personated her and gave him such a drubbing as he has never forgotten. He believes in her now, whilst the personator for a while dreaded her wrath at his pranks!

She walked there when one side of the hill was a green paddock, enclosed by palings; she walked after the paddock became a walled garden, probably she still walks when anyone lives in the big house; for I believe her to be caused by the light from the house (or the moonlight) reflected off a long double flagging leading to the front door, wavering as the gate moves in the wind – but it is a thankless task to expose a ghost to be a fraud.

Should you not wish to pass the church on your evening walk, you can go along the terrace, a high wide path at the top of the hill, on which part of the town is built.

Soon you are abreast of a pretty little house, with a garden in front, and some tall chimneys, *with cowls* at each end. Here once lived a 'character', a miser, I believe, who was found dead under peculiar circumstances (I think his name was Baxter, but cannot be sure), and therefore he groans at night. Indoors you hear nothing of it, but as you pass the house the groans are said to be most distressing. Schoolboys who, if they had known it, had a private ghost at the school, always went home the longer way, through the town, sooner than hear that groaning; and big fishermen would do a great deal to avoid it! That the chimney cowl was a fiction in the case, was an idea utterly scouted by all the wise, who maintained the ghost had existed before cowls were invented.

Having passed this terror, you would find the town steps on your left hand, and a patch of allotment on your right, after which you would reach a large house, in its own grounds, called by the name of an ancient family,[84] which, distinguished for beauty, wit, and gambling had lost all its land in the place, with a very trifling exception – if I remember rightly. For years, while their big house lay empty and half 'ruinated', as the folk there have it, a ghost, said to be of one De C—,[85] who met with a violent end, haunted the place, terrifying all who passed by. Lights were seen in the window places, and that when no one could have lived in such a den. By and bye it was rebuilt as a

---

[84] Crespigny House.
[85] De Crespignys.

school,[86] and the ghost was no more seen, but there lingered a sort of second-hand flavour of delicious horror about, as a house that *had* had a ghost.

---

[86] In 1870 Crespigny House was acquired by the school that later became Orwell Park School.

14

Squire Tempest.

The speaker was a cobbler, smooth shaven, if indeed Nature had ever required him to use a razor, dark-eyed, wiry, and spare, with a singular habit of crossing one wrist over another as he spoke, as though resting on an invisible prop, with a very rapid utterance.

"Oh! yes," he was saying, "things was awful in those days, when old Lord S——, father of him what's so high in Gov'ment, used ter live up at little Casino, yonder. Why, Squire Youghal, when he come, he thought he hadn't garden 'nuff, and 'twixt him and Parson Mayfield he contrived so's to git right a lot o' the charchyard into his graounds. I was a snip of a boy at that taime; and, oh! 'twas awful. Why! there was bits of legses, and bits of boneses, ay, and sculls and that together, all over that there bit o' garden, where them steps was, as went over th'wall into the churchyard."

"Why, that there well – you remember that well – oh! I wouldn't drink none on it – that stand right in a middle of all them there dead critturs – oh! I say, that's shocking!"

This lively description applied to the back garden of the house in which I had been brought up, though of this the cobbler was ignorant; and the water of that well, with its beautiful bubbles, had been the joy and stolen delight of my childhood, covered as it always was, by a square iron-ringed stone slab, which made me believe it must be a sort of Aladdin's stairway, artfully filled in with water.

I tried to turn his gruesome current into livelier strains, but in vain. "Passon Mayfield, now," he went on, "oh! he was a customer! beat his wife regular, and she a pretty little body as ever I set eyes on, but he and Squire Tempest they were a pair, they were; they used to set and drink till all's blue. They wasn't always friends, though – oh, no!"

It is impossible for words to express the look by which these impetuously uttered interjections were invariably accompanied; the effect was much as if an Egyptian mummy, one of those recently unrolled and photographed, had hypocritically raised deprecatory glances to an offended Heaven. He seemed, in telling his wild old stories, to force by this expression an assurance of his own superior and ever-to-be-relied-on propriety of action, thought, and demeanour.

"Squire Tempest, he'd a wife, a pretty slip she was too, till, what with him gaming and smuggling, and getting drunk, she got fare wore out; then he got sick of the sight of her, shut her up in the round turret, at the south end of the house, and took away the ladder, except when he remembered to send her some food. By and bye, she died; oh! poor critter; *that* was a mussy.[87] And Squire Tempest, he up and brought the body in from the turret, and has a splendid funeral – *splendid*, that that was. I was there a-looking on, I was; and that was fine – silver handles, and velvet pall, and plumes to the horses, and hat bands – oh, dear! So they took her to the church, for to bury her in the fam'ly vault, and then Passon Mayfield he up and says as how they can't bury no one without a-paying of him a fee or some'ut. 'That there vault that's just under where you sat a Sunday last. I see you goo up into the pew and sit there, right over.'"

---

[87] 'Mussy': mercy.

"So they come to words over it, and Squire Tempest, he use some awful language he do, and get his wife put decent into the vault, and all closed up, and that."

"Howsomedever, Passon Mayfield he warn't one to be diddled no-how, not he; so him and the sexton they come on the night, and they up with the coffin and puts it on the Holy Table. Oh! to think of it, why 'twas shocking, *shocking!* I see it myself, I did! I couldn't goo to church not then, not with *that* a-lying on the Holy Table. There worn't no East winder then, only a gloomy sort of owd picter of Moses and some others, a-standing there like morecombes (East Anglian – scarecrows),[88] enough to fright you into a fit, let alone putting the poor lady there."

"The coffin was there more'n three Sundays. 'Twas disgraceful. Everybody cried 'shame!' on 'em both, and nobody what could help it ud goo nigh the church. Howsomedever, I s'pose the Bishop or someb'dy hard of it, however that be. At last Squire Tempest, he up and pays the fee, or whatever that was that Passon Mayfield had the right to – and Passon he buried Mrs. Tempest back again to her proper place. Then people went to church again – they *could* yer know then! Passon Mayfield he reckon hid come it ove Squire this time, he did – so he went and had a silver mug made – and took it to his wif'. 'May,' says he, 'here's a present for you,' for all he did beat her awful – and on the mug was engraved these words as I now tell you –

'Mary, dear Mary, the Tempest is o'er!'"

---

[88] Painted figures of Moses and Aaron often flanked the Commandment Boards bearing the Ten Commandments that were a near-universal feature of all parish churches before the systematic reordering of churches in the Victorian gothic revival.

15

Squire Springfield.

Squire Tempest, however, was by no means alone with Parson Mayfield in eccentricity of character and in oddity of life.

Everyone who knows the sea coast of East Anglia, has heard of Squire Springfield and Squire Turnham, both of whom lived in the same village by the sea, at about the same date.

Squire Springfield belonged to an old family, which, in some curious way held its Orthorp[89] property, and in turns with another, equally old and equally distinguished. Each family held it for one lifetime only, a fact which prevented anything in the nature of an improvement from being set on foot, at least at the remoter time of which I am speaking.

Squire Springfield was middle aged when he came into possession, and he either built, or altered for himself, two curiously designed shooting-boxes, one near the shore, the other about four miles inland near the river, in the heart of a beautiful pine wood.

In the former, were one splendid reception room on the ground floor, and two small octagonal rooms at each end – the

---

[89] There is no such Suffolk village; James's choice of name may refer to Orford, Hollesley (another river close to the River Ore) or one of the villages along the River Orwell between Ipswich and the sea.

strange part of the arrangements consisting in the fact that the doors were all concealed, or almost concealed, by being made to open out of the corners of the rooms, each doors being shaped to shut into the corner, so that, in some cases, when open it looked like a three-winged screen.

Nor was this all – the walls were all panelled, and most of the panels opened by springs – the pedestals of the statuary opened in like manner, even the shutter cases were hollow, and could be opened by those who knew the secret.

As a child I have cried bitterly at being unable to find an exit from this large room, so artfully concealed were all but the folding doors at each end, which were unusually locked. In a passage behind the salon was a flag-stone, which lifted up, and showed a wooden stairway, now out of repair – which led to a complete and very well appointed suite of rooms below ground, lighted only by sunk lights, like cellars.

There was, however, little need of the sun's good offices, for the Squire lived by the artificial light of wax candles.

He began his day at eight in the evening, and went to bed at eight in the morning!

No one ever saw him by the full light of day, and even his lawyer's visits were made to him at night.

About nine or ten o'clock he would sally forth, and go to the other end of the town, where, in a humble pilot's house, lodged a lady, whose attire was wholly black: "even black linen, my dear," my informant (the pilot's daughter) would say.

To her, whose sobriquet of Black Miss Murbery was the only name by which she was ever known in the village, he never failed to pay a nocturnal visit; her habits of turning night into day being the same as his own. A poor woman once met him unexpectedly, on his way to Miss Murbery, and startled out of her good manners, she exclaimed, "Oh! Lord, sir, I thought it had been the devil." "No, no, Mrs. Wilkinson," he replied, in the peculiarly suave voice for which he was noted, "not just yet, not just yet!"

Attached to his house were some specially fine stables, with loose boxes for upwards of twenty horses, never used I believe; and many years after his death, when these were being cleared out, in the heart of an Augean muckheap was found a beautiful Italian monument to a lady of his family, with inscription, etc., all complete – which may now be seen in the parish church. Other curiosities were also found and handed to their rightful owners, the member of that other family which alternated with his until a short time ago.

Of a multitude of legends connected with Squire Springfield, it is best to say nothing; but I may be allowed to tell how, rising at his usual evening hour and going to the front door to draw a breath of dew-cooled air, he found a wee girl baby lying there. "Poor heart!" said he. "Poor heart! take it in, take it in," and this was done. The baby, whose origin was well guessed (though never supposed to be his own child), grew to womanhood as Miss Hart, and married, and lived in the other shooting-box in the wood, with husband and niece, till she died – many years after her kind protector had left his bat-like existence for another, where, let us hope, he longer shrinks, as on earth, from the full light and the open heaven.

16

Squire Turnham.

I tell these tales as they were told to me; this, then, must be the excuse for the abruptness or inconsequence of some of them – and, for the incompleteness of some of them – and, for the incompleteness of others, I must plead that those are now living who might be hurt by the setting down in print of much that is talked of and well known. So much on account of Squire Springfield's history – now to come to Squire Turnham, in whose case these restrictions cease to be effective.

"I knew very little of Squire Turnham; he was a good master to me; but I was allays in the kitchen," said the last person who had known him personally; but from many others, whose parents had known him, I have heard of him times and oft.

He was the younger brother of a well-known Roman Catholic nobleman, and when he came to Orthorp he set about building him a roomy and sufficiently stately mansion, within large grounds, and facing the sea.

He enclosed in it two existing cottages, possibly on the score of economy, and he either built or altered an underground passage between his own house and that of Lord S—— on the other side of the road, and at the top of the hill, below which his own was planted.

In this house were fine cellars and a large servants' hall below ground, and nearly all round the roof was a passage, in parts of which a six-foot man may stand erect and move freely; this was entered by tiny doors, concealed by furniture and by the paper hangings, and, no doubt, served to hide the spoils of many a midnight 'run' of smugglers, for whom this part of the coast was noted.

While the building was in progress, he would watch it day by day, and often, on seeing the growth of it would say: "*Very* nice! *Very* nice! pull it down and do better;" at which rate, it may be guessed, the house progressed but slowly.

However, when completed, it was thoroughly well built, and is now a model of good and thorough workmanship.

One room was decorated with a square shaped lattice of many battens, crossing each other at intervals of six or eight inches, and in this room – called the banqueting-room – the Squire kept a strange collection of wax figures, a sort of 'ragged regiment,' and of statuary, which it was 'quite the thing' to come and see if permission could be obtained.

From time to time the strange old man (who was not mad) had the room completely decorated with flowers – at what cost one can hardly imagine; and then, a fine supper being laid in the dining-room, he would stand at the door with his secretary and receive his guests. Grim, ghostly visitors, for the most part, for *no one ever came*, and most of those whom he would present to his secretary had been dead long since and more than half-forgotten!

The wretched secretary had to conduct these invisible 'convives' to the dining-room, and, leaving them to the silent intercourse which was all they could enjoy, had then to return to his master and the wax figures, and begin the same thing over again.

A man's nerves need to be iron to stand such a strain; and it is not wonderful was not seldom a new one.

I have seen the sale-bill including some of the wax figures, which have often been described to me.

This gentleman, too, preferred night to day, and is said to have been the original of the character of 'Paul Pry,' rendered famous by Liston and Toole.[90]

With a large umbrella tucked under his arm, no matter what the weather, he would go out at night and visit the tradesmen and pilots of the place at an hour when they would be thinking of bed.

He would bow deeply on gaining admittance, and in a small and oily voice would never fail to remark, "I *hope* I don't intrude" (pronounced intr*e*de), and would then prolong his visit far into the night. Yet, such was the charm of his manner and conversation, that no one resented his 'intr*u*sion.'

One of his nocturnal habits was to drive out into the country in his coach, accompanied by his secretary, and then, when some miles from the village, he would say as they went down some particularly sandy lane, "Mr. Secretary, it is raything heavy for the horses, don't you think you had better get out and walk?" A suggestion of this kind being equivalent to a command, I have often pitied the secretary stumbling homewards in the darkness, at the mercy of any smugglers who might meet him!

At last the old man died, and not yet were his eccentricities ended, for by his desire, his body lay in state with face uncovered, in the dining-room, with tall tapers burning, and the public admitted to gaze. The funeral took place at night, and though the churchyard wall bounded his garden, the singular old man was carried all along by the shore, through the pine clump meadow, and round to the church – quite a mile-and-a-half – when he was finally buried in a semi-feudal manner, that reminds one of the old customs of the great nobles of the North, with whom he was closely connected by blood.

---

[90] John Lawrence Toole (1830–1906) was an actor famous for his portrayal of the eponymous character in John Poole's farce *Paul Pry* (1825). 'Toole' here is probably an error for Poole.

Naturally, ghosts haunted the house that had held him, and naturally they chose the best rooms, but as they have never been known to do any harm, no one had any objection to their presence; and thus, no doubt, "they are there to this day."

17

Miss Waterton.

That little house in the High Street of Falston[91] has in it only one tiny room and an ante-room.

It was the scene of the most touching devotion in the early part of the present century, for there lived and sacrificed herself a high-born lady – but the story is best told from the beginning, thus –

Miss Waterton was the beautiful, self-willed, and somewhat spoiled daughter of a great nobleman – great – that is by reason of his lands and lineage – his title was not so lofty, but his station was unquestionably high. He was a patron of all the arts, more chiefly of the dramatic art and its votaries.

Often he would invite distinguished or promising actors to stay with him and enjoy the renowned hospitality of his country house, and the pleasant and cultivated society of the neighbourhood; which, for a country district, was somewhat wider in range than is usual, even at the present day.

Amongst those who had the opportunity of making the acquaintance of his daughter was a certain well-known young actor, called Jocelyn, who was a frequent visitor, and one who

---

[91] Falston, i.e. 'false town', a name to conceal the real name of the place.

was admitted to a closer intercourse with the actual family circle of his host than the rest of his confraternity.

He made a great impression on the heart of the young lady, and eventually had the astonishing temerity to propose for her hand!

She accepted him, and the affair was to have been kept secret, but in some way or other her father got knowledge of it, and sternly forbade any such idea, reproaching the young artist with the base return he had made for the hospitality that had been extended to him, and his daughter with the lapse from dignity she had shewn in permitting a clandestine engagement.

She made little complaint, but she pledged herself to her lover, then a heart-broken man, that never would she be the bride of any other man, and she kept her vow.

How hard a lot must have been hers it is difficult to realize, for every kind of pressure was brought to bear upon her, and match after match was brought forward, but in vain – her constancy, and possibly her pride, never faltered.

When the old lord, her father, died, she was still comparatively young, but although very poorly provided for, and although her brother, the heir, refused utterly to allow her a home in his family unless she would relinquish all idea of her lover, she remained form, – ay! even when the news was brought to her that her quondam lover had married, and she knew she had sacrificed herself for a semblance and a shadow!

So poor was she, that she came to live in the tiny tenement I have mentioned, where she was often visited by old and faithful friends.

There came a day when a band of travelling players arrived in the town; Miss Waterton was now over fifty, and old and broken for her age.

Amongst the names on the bill was that of Jocelyn, a 'come-down,', truly, for the once successful London actor! Miss Waterton went to see the performance, and came away sick at heart to see what time and self-indulgence had made of her idol, whose feet of clay were now, but all too visible!

In a few days the company left the little town, but not the actor Jocelyn – he was taken ill, and was ruthlessly left behind by the manager, who, having got the company together greatly by his aid, had got from him all he could, and left him sick and penniless, without compunction.

"The birds of the air carried the matter," and Miss Waterton heard of it; heard, too, how the faithless wife had, in his sorest need, deserted her husband, and strong in her noble forgiving devotion, she went to the wretched lodging where he lay who had wrecked her life – went, and came not away alone. She took back Jocelyn to her tiny house, gave up her bed to him, gave up her every comfort, using the ante-room herself, and nursed him uncomplainingly for the few years that yet remained of his wasted life.

Her friends were beside themselves at the scandal! – they reasoned with her, argued, talked, preached, scolded, and, in most cases, forsook her; but she said only, "I have loved him all my life, and have waited for him; we are old now, and I have a right to take care of him;" and she continued her loving ministrations, undeterred by all that might be urged.

He had acquired habits of intoxication, and had become hopelessly selfish and unthankful; rarely did her give her a kind word; rarely did he do aught but grumble at her, for luxuries which she could not procure; but once and again he would revert to the old days and the old ways, and in these flashes of lovers' love she found her satisfaction, only praying he might die the first – for well she knew if she were taken, the workhouse would be his last home on earth.

Her loyal, loving wish was granted, and grateful at last, bowed down by her enveloping, all-embracing love, he died in her arms; and with him she buried her life's romance, and lived peacefully on for a few years, till she, too, died and was buried, and almost, though not quite, forgotten. Not quite, for some few live who never forget such devotion, and to whom Miss Waterton's memory is as that of a saint.

18

Mary Broom.

If I were to tell all the romantic stories of my district, I should fill a book, and be thought to have dipped my pen in an inkwell of fiction! whereas, I should be relating true stories so like fiction, as rarely to be seen out of the pages of novels.

So I must tell the story of Mary Broom, with as few words as may be. She was a very pretty girl, the daughter of a dressmaker, who employed a good many other young women, all of whom still have a good word to say for Mary, in spite of her singular good fortune.

"She was as pretty as a picture, and quiet and that, and never said but very little," said one of her fellow apprentices, in talking of her not long since.

I remember her but vaguely, but I distinctly remember her mother; and I remember, too, the weird smell of the shiny linings and the extraordinary multitude of pins that seemed necessarily to associate themselves with the visits of the said Mrs. Broom.

For some reason Mary left the maternal work-room, and became maid to a lady of title, and, more than that, a lady of noble mind and kindly disposition, with whom she was very happy and much valued.

She kept a little 'to herself,' as folk say, and used her opportunities for reading well, also learning to speak without any sing-song in her accent, and to use the correct language of her mistress and the young ladies.

They were not beautiful, and she was, strikingly so; and it befell that when their brother came back from college he fell in love with her, and refused to give her up.

His parents with singular wisdom offered to send her to school, when, if he persisted in his fancy, they promised to give their consent, and this was agreed to. Her mother was sent for, and was told of the high prospects of her daughter, due not alone to her loveliness, but to her dignity of character and refinement; and after the period of probation was over, Mary and lover were married.

Her lady mother-in-law introduced her, thus hushing in her presence, at least, any insolence of the great world which she entered, and did not shrink from visiting the birthplace of her humble daughter.

When Mary's mother came to town, was an honoured guest; and when a fell disease laid its hands on her, it was to Mary's town house she was taken, and in Mary's arms she died.

I saw Mary, not many years back, at a railway station, waited for by a nobleman, and eagerly sought by many whose names are amongst the highest in the land, not only for birth, but for brains; and she was then, as no doubt she is still, a lovely typically English beauty, with no trace of rusticity about her.

The beauty of East Coast girls when Mary was young, and even after, was remarkable, and the children were sometimes as exquisite as any in a painter's fancies, though now-a-days the standard of good looks is far below what it was in those days.

As a pendant to the story of Mary Broom, though of a less agreeable nature, let me tell of the summer visitor to Orthorp, who fell in love with a fisherman.

Splendidly handsome he was, but in all book learning entirely ignorant, though honest and simple-minded enough.

She used to drive about with this caged Neptune beside her, and eventually she took him to London, where they were married, and, to all appearance, lived happily ever after.

His friends were always welcomed at her house, and though she was many years older than the husband of her choice, she never showed any jealousy or any desire to restrict his freedom; whilst on his part, I am credibly informed, her gave her a loyal and hearty affection.

Such things as these are indeed strange, but "Custom or not," as Mephistopheles says, "it happens though!"

19

The Beach King.

The man to whom this sobriquet belongs is one of the handsomest young fellows that ever sailed a boat, and comes of a handsome stock; only, whereas most of his family are fair and sturdy, he is as dark as a Spaniard, unusually tall, and with a head so set on his shoulders as to remind one at once of the old Greek statues.

His father is a noted swimmer, and has saved five lives in his time, besides acting as a coxswain of the life-boat for many years. Now in his old age he has invested his savings in a set of bathing machines, which are highly patronised by the summer visitors to Shingleborough,[92] partly on account of the old man's reputation for bravery, partly on account of the striking appearance of his son, who is always in charge.

Indeed, if Henry were not a little deaf, his head would by now have been fairly turned by the admiration openly expressed on all sides; and as it is, he is quite aware that his fine appearance has a good deal to do with the great success of the bathing machine venture.

---

[92] Shingleborough: almost certainly Aldeburgh, famed for its shingle beach, and where Ward was a common surname in the nineteenth century.

Who first gave him his name no one knows, but everyone justifies it by constant use, and probably there are many of the summer visitors who know him by no other.

In a fishing place where there are but few surnames, there are always numberless quaint nicknames in ordinary use, which, till one knows the reason for which they were first given, often sound supremely absurd – though no one can deny the great convenience of some such manner of distinguishing between four or five cousins all of the same name. 'Hawkeye,' 'Horky,' 'Ripper,' 'Gooseberry,' 'Whampo,' and 'Mariner,' are specimens of some of these nicknames; whilst the one surname of Ward is so common in the place that a little girl once asked as a riddle, "Why is Shingleborough so like a Hospital?" The answer being obviously, "Because it has so many 'Wards' in it."

Amongst the fishermen early marriages are the rule, but Harry at eight-and-twenty was still single, and the pretty girls in his own station of life began to think he never meant to marry, and to be furious with the ladies, who, they said made such a fuss of Harry, that he could not bring himself to think of one of his own sort.

The real fact was, that Harry had rather higher notions of what married life should be, than were common to his set, and this had prevented him from marrying without falling in love.

But no one can hope to escape the little god[93] – and the most we can ask is to be allowed to get it over young, and not make fools of ourselves in our maturer years.

Harry's turn came at last, and this was the manner of it. The summer bathing season of 187– had just come to its height, and Harry had need of all his tact and patience to arrange for everyone who wanted to bathe from his machines, so that each should have a fair time in the water, and that none should oust others by staying in too long, in resisting appeals of "Oh, do give me just one more lesson," from fair swimming pupils, and in

---

[93] Cupid.

politely hurrying the slow dressers, the pleasure of whose dip must one would think be sorely spoiled by the immense time they consume in the hot little machine before they dare re-appear in the eyes of the beach-world.

One morning he was feeling, as he expressed it, "fairly past his patience," and very glad to think that as it was nearly one o'clock, his morning's work, the worst in the day, would soon be over, when, as he toiled round and round the capstan, drawing up his machines, there came towards him a very pretty young woman.

At first he did not see her, and it was not until she tripped and nearly fell over the writhing rope, half in and half out of the stones, that, as he hastened to help her up, he looked in her sweet face, and – lost his heart.

She might have been a lady, or even a countess, it would (as indeed he thought at the first dawn) have made no difference to Harry. She was his love from that instant.

It was a case of 'love at first sight.'

"Oh!" she said, when she had recovered her stumble, looking at her pretty fresh pink cotton all stained with greasy iron rust, "dear, dear, what a horrid mess to get in, the very first time I set foot on the beach. I'm sure though I'm much obliged to you for helping me."

"Don't name it, miss," said Harry, feeling deeply grateful to the cause of the trip-up, which had brought him in speaking terms with this delightful creature.

"There now," she went on, looking at the path, the broad walk at the top of the beach, "here comes my mistress" (blessed word! then she *wasn't* a lady), "and I've never asked you for a machine for her yet. Oh, have you got one empty? and can you give her a swimming lesson? Quick! quick! please answer, or she will be so vexed with me."

"There will be one ready in a minute, miss," he answered, and collecting the clean towels and his mop he hastened to the door of a machine and knocked more vigorously than usual, saying, "Now then, mum, here's a lady waiting for a machine, and really I shall have to charge for two bathes, if you do keep it so long, mum."

The door opened suddenly, nearly knocking Harry off the springy board, and in great indignation out sailed a very stout, elderly, young lady, who was perhaps passable in the afternoon, when in all her bravery of paint and borrowed locks she paced the pier, but who at this moment looked more like one of Leech's caricatures[94] than anything mortal.

"I am astonished at you, Holland," she said, with great severity. "I am a regular customer, and have sent you a great many others, but for the future," this with an air of great dignity, so far as dignity and wet hair are compatible; "for the future I shall bathe elsewhere. Sarah! collect my towels and bring my dress home, don't stop to wring it, but bring it as it is," and trembling with indignation the offended lady sailed off the beach, followed by the unfortunate Sarah, whose hopes of one day making an impression on the insensible heart of the Beach King were now for ever quenched. The dripping bathing gown wept salt tears as she departed, with which not a few of her own were mingled.

Harry cared not one jot. The offended lady was well known as 'Old Troublesome' to the beach-men, who declared that if she wanted a bath, or fish, or what not, well as she paid, she never paid enough for the trouble her fidgety, worrying ways, gave to them.

Like magic, he cleared the machine, and hastened to the lady, who was a pleasant-looking woman, not very young, and who was as much struck as everyone else with the remarkable physical beauty of this young sea-dog.

The pretty maid thanked Harry, in a low voice, for being so quick, and he was just going to ask her whether she got out of an evening, when her mistress called, "Lucy, I shall want you, as

---

[94] John Leech (1817–64) was the leading caricaturist of *Punch* magazine in the early years of the publication.

it is so late;" and saying, "Good-bye! and thank you, I'm sure," off she ran.

She was a most discreet damsel, and for several days she would not enter into anything like conversation with the Beach King, who, poor fellow, was so completely her slave, that he thought of nothing but how he should persuade her to let him keep company with her, while as yet he knew only her Christian name.

Fortune favours the bold, they say, and sometimes truly. One evening the mistress and her husband had gone out for a sail with Harry's father, and Lucy came down to the beach to see them start.

"How are you, miss, this evening?" said Harry, as soon as the boat was fairly off.

"Oh, la! now you did startle me, Mr. Holland," she replied. "Why, I am very well, and very busy, and I can't stay here talking to *you*," and she tried to slip past him off the stones.

Harry was used to be admired and almost sought after by the girls he knew, and, therefore, this behaviour of Lucy's only increased his determination to know her.

He stepped in front of her as if by accident, and looking full at her with his keen dark eyes, said, "Won't you go for a turn with me along the Path? I'll take care of you, you know."

Lucy wanted to go with all her heart, but she "wasn't sure – her mistress mightn't like it, and she ought to go and see Annie." Annie was maid to Lucy's mistress' sister-in-law.

"Well," said Harry, "let me see you down to Annie's." Then, as she began to refuse, he said, "What have I done or what have you heard against me that you won't speak to me, and won't look at me? I tell you, Miss Lucy – meaning no offence, but your other name I don't know – if you won't let me walk alongside of you, I'll walk behind you, and I'll wait till you go home, and walk behind you again."

Just at this moment Annie came down on to the beach, and being an old acquaintance of Harry's, she soon set Lucy's mind at ease about the walking together, and for this night they went all three in a party; a very nice arrangement, but by no means all Harry could have wished.

However, now the ice was broken, and the passionate, sudden love of Harry's heart poured itself out right lavishly on Lucy. She had bathes for nothing, when ladies were clamouring for a machine, kept empty till she could come. She went for sails when rich people had offered double for the boat's hire. Everything he could do for her to spare her trouble he did; and everything he did she accepted as a matter of course, for though she was in love with him, her love was a very different thing from his.

She was very well educated, being, as she told her lover, an only child, and had come to service solely because she was so fond of her mistress, who was her godmother, and she wanted to see a little of the world before settling down.

Annie told her nothing but good about Harry, and in every way he was an excellent match for her. She liked the seaside life, and she liked Harry's bluff old father, who, for his part, was never weary of pointing her out as "that pretty gal o' Harry's."

He chuckled now and then to see the offended airs of some of Harry's lady customers, when they noticed his admiration for the pretty maid, whereby his indifference to them was greatly increased.

Lucy Willis was at Shingleborough for several weeks of the season, her mistress staying on long after the summer had ended; for Shingleborough in the autumn is far pleasanter than in the hot weather, and St. Luke and St. Martin each do their utmost with their 'little summers,'[95] as Mrs. Blandy knew of old.

Harry and Lucy Willis were walking together one day when he asked her, after a somewhat lengthened silence, "Lucy,

---

[95] A reference to the warmer days ('little summers') that sometimes occur around St Luke's Day on 18 October and St Martin's Day on 11 November.

when will you be my wife?" Lucy started as if she had been struck, and grew very pale, answering, "Oh, don't ask me; don't ask me!" "Why, my dear," he said, gently; "when I asked you to go to that sale with me, and help me choose them bits of furniture, you knew right well whose room they were meant for; didn't you, now?" Lucy could only nod her head for "Yes;" and Harry went on, "when I said didn't you think there was room enough for more to live along o' father and me, you said 'Yes'; and you *knew* who I wanted there to be room for?" Lucy, who was now as crimson as before she had been pale, whispered "Yes." "Then," said he, almost sternly, it was such a real matter to him, "did you go on letting me love you, and thinking you loved me back, and all the while you did not care a halfpenny." "No! no! no!" she cried, "I love you, I love you; but oh, I'm afraid." "Afraid," said Harry, in a curious, half-proud, half-astonished tone.

"What can you have to be afraid of – do you think I shall be a bad 'un to you?" "No," she said; "oh, no, Harry – but I am afraid." A horrible dread crossed Harry's mind for one instant, he knew very little of Lucy's life before he had made her acquaintance at Shingleborough. Could there be any secret in her past that she wished to hide? – but, no, it was impossible to know her as he did and harbour such a doubt.

"Tell me what you are afraid of," he asked. "Anyhow it isn't me now, is it?" he added, with a little nervous laugh.

"No," she said, "it isn't you, Harry; it's my father and altogether, and those at home."

"Your father! why I thought you said he was so fond o' you, and made so much of you!"

"Yes, oh, so he does! but there, Harry, I'm right down afraid to tell him. I know he will be so angry."

"Well, why should *you* tell him," said her lover; "leave that to me. I'll not write, but I'll go and see him, and he'll see I'm anyhow big enough to take care of you."

"No, *no*, Harry! promise me not to go and see father till I tell you," she cried; "promise me faithfully."

Harry was dreadfully puzzled; he saw no way of quieting her evident terror but by making the desired promise, to which, however, he added, as a condition, that if she sent him no word from Christmas to Easter forbidding him to come, then, promise or no, he should come to London and ask for her at her father's hands.

"So you must get your things together all ready, my dear," he said, "and keep up a brave heart; and if I'm the Beach King, why I will make a Beach Queen of you!"

"Oh! Harry," she answered, blushing, "there! how you do talk, to be sure. I shall be glad when Easter comes," she said, "for then all the worry'll be over: you know I *do* love you, don't you?" she added. "You'd knock down anyone that doubted it, wouldn't you? You'll believe it, whatever happens? promise, whatever happens!"

"There's no call for me to promise such a thing as that," he said. "If I could misdoubt you, the love wouldn't be worth much to either of us, besides, I can read writing, if 'tis writ plain, and you are going to write to me, aren't you?"

"If I can," she said, "but maybe I shan't be able to, and that's what I mean; you must trust me, whatever you hear from others, and even if you don't hear anything from me."

'Well! I don't like these sort of waiting ways,' said Harry. "I'd a deal better have it out with your father, and know the end of it, bad or good; but if you say, 'won't,' why, 'wait's' the word, and if you say 'trust,' why, there it is, you see."

He was not quite satisfied with this curious conversation, and often turned it over in his mind, especially after Lucy and her mistress had left Shingleborough, which they did early in December; Lucy to go home to her father, as soon as her mistress got back to the garrison town, where she and her husband were stationed.

He saw her off, and "dang it!" he said, half angrily to himself afterwards, "I never felt such a fool in my life – with Lucy's mistress looking the other way on purpose, and Lucy with tears in her eyes – there, well I've got to do the waiting now, and precious hard that'll fare to be."

A beautiful card arrived for him at Christmas from his "ever-loving Lucy Willis," but no letter.

The slow weeks wore on towards Easter, and though he wrote once or twice to Lucy, never a word did she send him in reply. Still he trusted her, and hoped the silence meant that he might act on his condition when the time came, and go to see her father himself.

He did bits of carpentering about the house, putting up shelves and a corner cupboard for her convenience. He holystoned[96] the floor of the upstairs room till it looked as white as the deck of a yacht; all the uneven boards he planed and fastened down that she might not hurt herself with splinters in scrubbing hereafter, and with thrums[97] of flag-mending wools he made one or two soft cushions.

Then he had a new suit of dark-blue clothes made for himself, and went to be photographed, the result being a very poor presentment of the handsome fellow whose beach attire with his collar open was far more suitable and becoming, though no doubt less conventional.

"If any of her people wonder what sort of a stick she's picked up with," he said to himself, "that'll show 'em," and he was more than ever reserved and grave with the girls in the place, who declared "for all, Harry was such a proper man, they didn't care for that sort that was so nasty stuck-up, and couldn't pass the time of day with old friends: all along of *strangers*."

He paid no heed to their jealous spite, but went on with the waiting, as he called it, though he was often almost sick with the excitement within him, and fretted almost beyond endurance by this trial of his patience and the heavy silence of his beloved,

---

[96] 'Holystoning': a nautical term meaning to scrub a ship's boards (or, in this case, the floorboards of a house) with a piece of sandstone.

[97] 'Thrums': unwoven threads at the edge of a piece of woven cloth.

aggravated as it all was by the constant questions and remarks of his old father, who had taken a strong liking to Lucy; and being very proud of his son, could not bear to see him "so downcast," as he said.

At last, at the long last, as it seemed to Harry, came Easter-tide – all the extra convenience of trips to London for four days – and no forbidding letter from his love.

He told his father he was off to London on the Easter Monday, and might be one day, or might be three, away. The old man chuckled, "Well, boy, bring her back along of you. We've all got a welcome of her here," he said. "Now then, father," said Harry, almost sharply, he was so strung up by excitement, "don't you go talking about my business out of this house, or you and I shall fall out." "All right, boy, all right," said the old fellow, good temperedly, "but you can take her my welcome, if that isn't too heavy for your pockets: ha! ha!"

In the train – which, though fairly quick for an excursion train, seemed to Harry, to crawl like a South Eastern 'parly,'[98] – his fine appearance attracted much notice, one fidgetty child, that had been the plague of the entire compartment, settling down opposite to Harry with wide delighted eyes.

"He's like Goliath, only he's so pretty," it said, whereupon there was a roar of laughter, in which Harry joined mechanically.

He took a cab and told the man to drive fast, utterly reckless of distance or expense.

The cabman took him at his word, and drove like a very Jehu,[99] till a policeman observing the break-neck pace, peremptorily ordered him to slacken, ay, and took his number;

---

[98] 'Parly': short form of 'Parliamentary train', a train run on a branch line in compliance with the Railway Regulation Act 1844 purely to keep the line open.

[99] The reference is to 2 Kings 9:20: 'The driving is like the driving of Jehu the son of Nimshi; for he driveth furiously'.

for all of which Harry's pocket had to act consoler. When at length they reached the house, where the man stared amazed at the reckless way in which his fare paid him his exorbitant demand, and never made the least demur. Harry gave a thundering knock, and such a pull at the bell as nearly startled the little maid into hysterics.

When she opened the door he began at once to go in, saying to the girl, "Your mistress, Lucy Willis, is at home, ain't she?"

"No," stammered the girl, "she is not; at least, not here, and I haven't heard she's come back to her home either, not yet." "*Back* to her home," repeated Harry; "back to her *home*! why where *is* her home, if it ain't here? Look ye here, my girl, I am not in a mood for none of your jokes and nonsense; nor I ain't going to put up with them. Just you go and tell Lucy that Harry Holland is here, a-waiting to see her before he goes in to see her father."

"But I *can't* tell her, sir. Oh lor don't hit me!" whimpered the girl, looking at his angry face. "I *can't* tell her; she isn't here, sir, indeed she isn't. She is away on her wedding trip!"

"Her *what*?" said Harry, in a voice of thunder; "don't I tell you not to fool with me."

"Oh lor, sir, I ain't a-fooling, not nohow. She's married, sir, and on her wedding trip."

His face was a fearful sight to see; he leant against the doorpost whilst the sweat stood in great drops on his brow. "Then *d–n* her," he cried, when he got back his voice, "d–n her and every woman like her," and in his rage of disappointed love and misery he cursed and swore most fearfully.

The little maid stood quaking in the entry not daring to do anything, so paralysed was she at the 'goings on' of this unknown young man. She wanted to call her master, but was afraid to leave the stranger half inside the doorway, and she feared to ask him to move whilst he leant there swearing as if he were mad or drunk, or both.

She was saved from having to do either, for the noise reached the ears of Mr. Willis, as he sat in his back room, where he finished the delicate instruments which he manufactured, and pushing up his spectacles on his forehead, he came out to see what was going on.

He was a small man, with those weak pink-edged eyes that look quite helpless and blinking, when they are not protected by glasses. His manner was abstracted and rather petulant. In fact, no greater contrast could have been found to Harry raging on the doorway, than this mild little being, the father of his love.

"What is all this about, Mary Anne?" began old Willis. "What are you doing here, allowing ruffians like this to get into my house? Why don't you call the police, girl? Why don't you lock the door? Why don't you send him away? Why –"

What more he was going to say was never known. Harry burst in with a furious exclamation of "Look here, old man, are you Lucy Willis's father?" And as he answered in the affirmative, Harry went on, whilst old Willis gasped and blinked, "Then you and I must have some words together. I may be a sea-faring man, but I ain't quite a soft, and I've got to know the meaning of all this."

"Well, sir," stammered old Willis, with a futile attempt at dignity: "it seems to me as if *I'd* a right to say the same. What do you mean by coming here where nobody knows you, and brawling on my doorstep for everyone to see! and for the matter of that, to hear? I'm a respectable tradesman, I'd have you to know, and I won't permit it."

The little man's speech was rendered almost ridiculous by this conclusion, for, as to 'permitting' or preventing Harry, he was quite powerless by reason of his small stature and general feebleness of build.

"Now, then, old man," said Harry, still angrily: "do you mean to say you never heard of me, Harry Holland; do you mean to tell me that your girl Lucy has gone and got married?"

"I do, sir; I do," said the old man all in a flutter, "and I can't conceive in what way it is your business."

"Oh, none of *my* business, none at all," sneered Harry, "only that Lucy was going to marry me! that's all my old cock."

"I think, sir," said Lucy's father with great self-control, "you had better come in an explain yourself, for I am at a loss to understand your words; and if you are to bring my daughter's name into the conversation, it had better not be in public: Mary Anne shut the door," as Harry strode into the house, and stalked up the entry after the old man, into his sanctum.

"Sit down, sir, sit down," said the old father, soothingly. "I hope we may come to an agreeable understanding."

His oily manner only irritated poor Harry, and he said, roughly, "I'll stand till I know the meaning of this, but I'll sit none in *your* house."

"Will you first explain to me the reason, I may say, the object, the intention, as it were, of your visit?" said Willis, in a fluttered, uneasy way.

"I came to see Lucy, and to ask her, from you, for my wife," was the plain-spoken answer.

"And how did you propose to, – er, gain my consent – er – young man? Lucy had been engaged for many years to the man she has, – er – married."

"Lucy promised herself to me last summer at Shingleborough," said Harry, "and I was to come for her at Easter. I've come, and what have I got? *Curse* her! What's her name? Where does she live? No! I ain't going to swing for her. I'm going to write to her, that's all. Only a nice little letter, to *congratulate*, you know," he sneered.

"Lucy never told me she had made your acquaintance, young man. She knew that she was not free to marry anyone but that man she *has* married, and no doubt that was why she did not speak of you."

"Was she in love with the man? Tell me that," said Harry, shortly.

"Well," hesitated the old father, "she was not what you may call outspoken in her feelings on the subject. In fact, she did not wish to have it come off so soon."

"Oh," said Harry. "Well, there's no good in talking about it. Just give me that address, and I'll rid you o' my presence. You don't seem to like me as much as most people do," he laughed.

The old man shakily wrote the address, and Harry took it, screwed it up into a little wisp, and put it safe in his envelope of photographs.

"You'll be moderate in what you say, moderate, I beg!" said the father, anxiously. "I suppose we must admit that you've been badly used, young man, but there's as good fish in the sea as ever came out of it, to speak after your own manner," he chuckled, fatuously.

"My manner anyhow isn't a fool's manner," said Harry, rudely, and he got up and stalked out of the house without another word. Poor fellow he was hit hard, and no mistake about it; his belief in women had received a shock it would take years to recover, if it ever did recover at all.

He turned into a coffee shop near, not that he was a temperance man, but he wanted a clear head and a quiet place to write his 'little letter.'

Having bought his paper and envelope and stamp, and secured a table to himself, he began to write – a long and wearisome business to his unaccustomed fingers.

Sheet after sheet he spoiled, but at last the letter was finished, and ran nearly as follows: –

"Harry Holland thanks Lucy Willis for her kind behaviour to him, and wish you as happy as you deserve to be in her married life. If Lucy have got anything to say to him, she knows where it will find me, and remain,

Yours *truly*, which is more than *she* can say,

HARRY HOLLAND."

Then he laid his head on his hands, and fell fast asleep with exhaustion, the untouched, untasted coffee at his elbow.

By-and-bye he was wakened by the attendant, who, seeing he had eaten nothing, persuaded him to have some food and some fresh coffee, after which he went slowly back to the station, and so home, with his sore heart and blighted hopes, to the village by the sea.

His father saw something was wrong, and with rare tact refrained from questioning him, but on the second day Harry came to him and said, in a would-be careless manner, "That's all off between me and her, father, and you'll oblige me not to speak of it any more."

His father growled out some sort of assent, and the two shook hands, but no words were passed on the matter.

On the third day came a London letter for Harry, a thick letter with two stamps, and even then a penny to pay. The postman tried to make some little joke about love being heavier than usual in this case; but he met such a fierce look from Harry, that his little bit of nonsense seemed to shrivel up before it, and he went away muttering, "'Beach King' is he! I'd 'king' him with his airs, I would."

The letter was, of course, from Lucy, who was a good hand with her pen; a heart-broken epistle, full of sorrow and entreaties for pardon at first, which so angered Harry, that he threw it down and went out.

When he came in and took it up, he gave a great start, the words he saw on turning the page were like a flash of lightning to his brain. "My father sold me in payment of an old debt. I was no freer than a black nigger slave," he read. "I told you I was afraid, and you only laughed at me."

He never laid down the closely written sheets till he had mastered the whole of their contents, then he burst out crying like a child, and sobbed, those terrible sobs of a man in agony of spirit; but he forgave Lucy, and this is why. In that thick letter she told him her story, which, but for the love that blinded her to his interest, she had better have told him that happy summer at Shingleborough then it might have been so different. It 'might have been'; but now it could never be helped, so he forgave her.

Lucy was, as we have said before, an only child; and her mother having died when she was very small, her father had done so much himself for the little creature that he became far fonder of her than fathers usually are of quite small children. When she was only three he began to speculate with a view to making a fortune for Lucy. Lucy was to be well educated; Lucy was to be made into a lady; Lucy was never to work.

He got on pretty well for a few years, but having very little money for these ventures, he found himself, at the first bad investment, crippled for the want of ready-money to carry on his lucrative but expensive instrument-making business. In his difficulty he applied to an old and trusted friend of his, a man but a few years younger than himself (a man of about five-and-thirty), for a loan or a mortgage to tide him over the troublous time.

The other man made him advances, not once, nor twice, but many times, and Willis at last retrieved his losses, but still had not succeeded in paying off the entire sum, when, through family circumstances, his friend, in turn, became pressed for a few hundreds, and reasonably and naturally applied to Willis for the unpaid balance of the loan.

Willis could not pay it, yet he was very loath to be made a bankrupt, and his friend was most unwilling to take strong measures, though his need was urgent.

He waited as long as he could. Willis honestly strove to collect the sum due, by the date fixed, but in vain.

On the day appointed for the payment, the friend came to Willis in his laboratory, and told him plainly that he could wait no longer; either he must be paid or he must make a bankrupt of him. There was no rancour between the men, but they were sitting in gloomy silence with some stiff grog before them, making from time to time some trivial remark, when the door opened, and Lucy, then eight years old, ran in to the work-room, straight to her dear daddy, as she called him, to show him some new treasure.

She was even then unusually pretty, and looked even more so than she perhaps was, from the sharp contrast of her child-like freshness with the two toil-worn men, and the dingy workroom with its odd smell of ever-burning gas.

The friend looked at her keenly with an observant eye that took in every detail of her charm, from her fluffy hair and winning fair little face, to her tiny nimble feet and caressing arms, and an idea came into his head.

Her father soon put her down with a heavy sigh, bidding her run away now, and not come back while daddy was busy, and the moment the door had banged behind the child, the friend began to develop his idea.

"John Willis," he said, "you know my credit is good."

"I do," replied the other. "I wish mine were as firm as yours is."

"You know why I want that money," continued the friend.

"Yes," said Willis, heavily. "What's the good of going all over it again? You want it, an' you've got to have it. That's settled."

"Well, but suppose after all I was to do without it? Or I don't mean do without it, for I must get it otherhow, if I don't have it from you. Suppose I was to forgive you the debt?"

"Suppose! Suppose! Suppose! Suppose this! Suppose that!" said Willis, testily. "What is the use of talking like that?"

"This is the use of it, man," his friend replied. "I make you the offer to forgive you the rest of the debt; to give you a writing duly witnessed, clearing you from all further liability, if you will give me a similar writing, signed and witnessed, promising to give me your daughter for a wife as soon as she's old enough, or as soon after she's grown up as I ask for her."

"The man's mad!" said Willis, half aloud. "How can I make bargains with my flesh and blood? I can't sell my own daughter; she may not like you when she grows up."

"But you must take care she does," said the friend, and his being a strong nature while Willis' was very weak, it was not long before the bargain was concluded.

Of all this Lucy knew nothing, and though she saw very few people except her father, the old servant, and this friend, she never took any interest in him beyond the natural liking of a lonely girl for the only person who ever gives her any presents, and she would slip away after thanking him, to avoid the kiss (without which he thought the thanks incomplete), and the long dull conversations which he held with her father in the winter evenings, when they both sat smoking by the fire.

Lucy was nineteen, and a very pretty girl, when her godmother, Mrs. Blandy, came to see them in London, and happening to say she must look out for a temporary lady's maid, awoke in Lucy's mind a keen desire to offer herself for the place. She knew all that would be required of her very well indeed, and was sure that her wish to see the world by going to service would never be granted by her father unless it were under such a mistress, so she begged Mrs. Blandy to ask Mr. Willis if she might go, and the lady, who had never thought of having such a refined superior servant, was only too glad to fall in with the plan. Willis gave his consent, and Lucy got ready to go.

The night before she was to start, in came the friend, who having been absent for a few days, had heard nothing of this plan. He was extremely angry when he was told.

"You don't consider," he said, "my right in this matter. I bought Lucy years ago for four hundred pounds, and now you talk of her going away as if you had not eyes to see the risk I run of losing her. Why she may be married before she comes back."

"Well, well," said her father, "we'll tell her before she goes," secretly thinking: "I can easily pay him back his dirty money now, thank goodness, and if he waits a little bit, she'll be of age, and no document that we have made can bind her." Alas! the same idea occurred to the friend, who suddenly asked what her exact age was.

"Nineteen-and-a-half," said the father, inwardly dreading what the friend would say next, which was –

"Then you will tell Lucy that she is to be married next summer. I can't run the chance of her refusing to be bound by those writings, if she once touches her one-and-twenty."

"Well, but if she don't like the idea," said her father deprecatingly, "would it be the same to you if I paid you the four hundred down."

"The same to me!" shouted the friend, "why, man! do you take me for a thing like yourself, that think flesh-and-blood and money all as one – don't dare to offer me your vile money – do you think I'm the devil, that you try to cheat me? – Lord, man," he said, "I *love* her!"

That last was a contingency that had never entered John Willis's head.

At supper that night, together with his friend and Lucy, John Willis gave his daughter a great deal of good and sound advice as to suitable behaviour in her new life: all that sort of advice which seems to the uninitiated in the ways of the world, first, so unnecessary, and, secondly, so "horrid," as they express it, "making everyone else out so bad." Lucy ventured on some such remark, whereupon the friend, nudging her father, said, "Now's the time to speak, tell her now."

Feeling, for the first time, since the fatal bargain was concluded, a full sense of the degradation it had heaped upon him, John Willis stood up, and looking away from Lucy, began to explain matters to her.

"You know," he said, "Lucy, that conduct that's all well and good for a free woman, is quite another thing if you're engaged, promised you know. You can't be too shy of everyone, you can't be too circumspect. Circumspect is the word, isn't it, Richard!" he said, appealing to his friend.

"Well, but father," said Lucy, "if circumspect is the word, I don't know what it means, so it's not much good to use it; and besides, I never do behave badly, now do I? and then *I'm* not engaged."

"Yes, you are, Lucy; yes, you are," he said, hurriedly, "ever since you were a little girl. Engaged to friend Richard, there, and to be married next summer."

"Well, of all I ever did," exclaimed Lucy, "this is the queerest thing – why, father, Richard is as old as you, and greyer too; besides, how do you know I'll have him?" she said, coquettishly.

Then the solemn Richard took up the word, and looking with some contempt on poor limp John Willis, who shifted uneasily from one leg to the other, with anything but a happy look, he said, "These are the facts of the matter, Lucy, and facts are stubborn things, as says the poet. Your consent, Lucy, is not wanting in this affair, my dear. 'Twas settled when you were but eight years old, between me and your father there, that in consideration of my forgiving him a large debt you were to be my wife when of full age. The documents say nothing of consent on your part; and – Lucy – I love you, my dear."

Lucy was very angry. "Do you, indeed?" she answered. "Then it's more than I do you. I'll tell Mrs. Blandy, and see what she'll say about it, I will indeed. Father! how could you do such a shameful, shameful, wicked thing. How could you?"

Both men hastened to insist that she should promise not to mention the compact to anyone, and at last she had to give in, or give up going with her godmother. This seeming to offer at least one chance to escape, she willingly gave her promise sooner than forego it.

"Oh, Harry!" the poor girl wrote, "why didn't you have our banns put up *then*, and marry me, but you never thought of it." No, he never had, and what is more, an underhand thing like that is what he never would have done. Men are so different from women, thank God.

"When you said you'd speak to father, I was terrified for fear he'd think I'd told you, and I trusted I'd be able to put off the marriage. I said I was ill, and so I was (all my colour's gone, Harry). 'Never mind! being married would be a change, and I'd soon be well,' they said. I said I must go to Mrs. Blandy, and a letter came saying I must wait a week; she couldn't have me. I did everything I could, and you never came, and I daren't write, for father and Richard took up the notion I'd got a lover, and at last Richard got fairly frightened, and on Easter he came with a license, £50 that cost him. Fancy me worth £50 more! And we were married then and there that blessed Easter day, and off we went to the Isle of Wight. I'm miserable, and Richard's miserable, and so's father, and so are you, Harry; but for pity's sake, Harry, forgive me" – here the letter was very much crumpled as if it had been snatched, and went on after a space too creased to write upon – "He'd read it all! Oh, Harry, and he's *beaten* me! and we only married on Monday, and this Thursday. I daren't say any more, but do think kindly of your broken-hearted

LUCY."

Well, as I said, he forgave her, and held up his head again, knowing that in her heart she had been true; but it was years before he made any friends again in the summer, and when he did, his choice fell on a grave, plain woman, not so young or so taking as Lucy, but whose sad home life made his heart soften to her; and by-and-bye she married him. They are very happy in a quiet way. They have two boys, who bid fair to rival their handsome young father in time. But the joy of his eyes and his heart's delight, is his little daughter Lucy.

20

Geordie, the Sea Waif.

A true story.

It was a fine morning in early autumn, the sea was just curling on the sandbanks in the bay with the fresh brisk north-east wind, the pilots were marching up and down the hard patch of ground by their 'look-out' station, watching for vessels which might need their services; some of the fishermen were mending and arranging their nets; and the women were hanging out their clothes to dry, on the lines near the beach; when, from a barque that was at anchor in the bay, a boat was seen to put off for the shore.

What could be amiss on board? was the question everyone asked at once, and "oh!" as the rowers drew nearer, "dear heart alive" said the women, "whatever is that in the bottom of the boat!"

With aprons shading their eyes, they eagerly watched the boat, till at last, she touched on the stony beach; and then, to the surprise of all, they saw the object in the bottom of the boat was a lad about thirteen years old, evidently badly hurt, and groaning in pain.

The four sailors who had rowed him to shore, now came forward, and told the fisherfolk that the poor little fellow had caught his foot the previous night in the boat's 'painter' (the rope by which one boat is secured to another), and had fallen and broken his thigh. They could not care for him as he must be cared for if he was to be cured, and they had no money to offer for his keep, but they brought the boy ashore in the hope that some kind soul, with lads of her own, would take him in and nurse him. It was a great deal to ask of such poor people as were all the crowd upon the beach, a great deal to expect, yet the men had plainly no doubt that a friendly heart would be found to undertake this strange charge, and their simple confidence was not mistaken.

As the bystanders thought over the matter in their minds (their hearts would all have said 'Yes'), a tall, handsome woman, with a red handkerchief on her dark, wavy hair, came quickly down to the water-side, and when she heard the sad story, she did not hesitate a moment, but out of her great kindly heart she spoke at once: "The Lord'll never let me be the poorer for it, give me the lad, men, and bring him along to mine – I'll take right good care on him."

"Bless you, mother," said the sailors, and borrowing a net stretcher from one of the fishermen, they gently laid the poor boy on it, and with the greatest care bore him off to the widow's cottage – for this brave-hearted woman was a widow, who had had the greatest struggle to rear her own four boys, but whose experience had taught her to believe that those who trust in God are never quite destitute.

She made up a little bed in her parlour, taking from upstairs that which belonged to her youngest son, and here the rough shipmates laid the boy tenderly, and bade him farewell. They had given him half-a-crown to let them bring him ashore, he screamed so at the idea of being moved, and this was nearly all they had for tobacco until they reached London; but the small remainder, about eighteenpence, they now gave him as a parting present, thus leaving themselves without any means of buying what, to a sailor, is almost more necessary than food.

"We shall miss the lad sorely, mother," they said. "Geordie Gray has been rare good company a-board. He can cook and sing, and dance and play the flute, and is a real biddable lad he is. Captain, he say he'll see if the owners'll do anything for them that take him in. But 'tis the boy's first voyage along of us, so there's not much chance of that."

"Well! farewell Geordie, lad," they added; "keep up heart, my lad, we won't forget ye;" and as Geordie clung sobbing to each of his rough friends in turn, the good fellows gulphed[100] and rubbed their eyes with their hard hands to keep away the unusual tears that gathered there.

He was a nice-looking little fellow, fair, with mischievous merry blue eyes and light hair, and the very broadest north country accent, so that at first it was hard for his kind nurse to understand him.

Just as he was settled, and the widow's youngest son had gone to fetch the doctor to set his thigh, a pretty young woman came to say that *she* would take the boy, for her husband was a sailor and in good earnings; and "she had no children," she went on, "and could better bear the expense. "Besides," she said, " I know how I should feel if my Sam met with an accident and was as helpless as this little Geordie here."

But, of course, the boy could not be moved again, and the widow would not have parted with him even if it had been possible. Both she and her two boys, then at home, seemed to have taken the sea-waif to their hearts, and to have loved him at once.

The doctor was out, and when he did come it was very dark, and the setting was so unsuccessful that next day it had to be done all over again.

By this time everyone in the little town had heard of the strange visitor, and of the widow's kind act in taking him into her house. Her confidence, that she would not suffer, was fully justified, for high and low, rich and poor, all came to bring help, in one way or another, some with dainty food, some with

---

100 I have been unable to trace the meaning of this dialect term.

bandaging, or changes of clothes and sheets, others to offer help and nursing by day and night, all interested, and all eager to share in the good work.

The broken thigh took a very long time to mend, little Geordie not being the best of patients as to keeping still. But when not in pain, he was a very amusing fellow, and soon wound himself into the widow's heart, so that she was delighted when he said, one day,

"Mother, if you'll let me be your real boy, when I get well, I'll work for you and bring you all I earn, and I'll be your own son always."

"Well, but, my dear," she answered, "haven't you got a mother of your own, that'll want you when you're well. Tell me how you happened to go to sea and all, and you so small too."

Then he told her his sad little story, which was proved upon inquiry to be quite true, and which ran as follows: –

When he was a very little boy he had a nice home and a little brother and sister. To this sister his heart seemed to go out more than even to his mother, fond as he was of her. But by-and-bye his father, who was a ship's carpenter and a clever workman, took to drinking. Gradually the comfort departed from the home, the poor wife enduring much in silence, for her uncle and only relation was a rising man, who owned several small trading vessels, and she could not bear that her trouble should be known to him.

"I *hate* my father," said Geordie, fiercely. "He hurt my little sister."

After a few years of the greatest misery, the father having betrayed his fatal failing to his wife's rich uncle, and not being able to get any work, one day deserted his family. Then the wife appealed to her uncle, who refrained from more than writing that he had always disliked and distrusted her husband, and said that he could not help her, because he felt quite sure the husband would come back if he saw any hope of living at someone else's expense. She must go to the workhouse with her children, at any rate for a while, and if the man did not appear to claim her in a given time, *then* he would try and help her.

This was hard, but justified by facts, as the wretched husband did come back and try to live on his wife's earnings for a while, again deserting her when no money was forthcoming.

Of their life in the workhouse, Geordie spoke with the greatest indignation. Certain hours of schooling must be gone through in accordance with the Act then in force,[101] which unfortunately did not specify what part of the twenty-four hours was to be devoted to the school work. As it happened, the master of this workhouse was a grasping, greedy man, who was able to employ the boys' labour in work for himself, which brought him in a fair amount of money. He, therefore, arranged the day's work in such a way, that the only time left for the compulsory schooling was after nine o'clock at thing.

Poor little lad; no wonder he resented such a life, even long after he had freed himself from it.

On one of his few days out, he went to see his uncle, and ask him to put him out to sea in one of his boats, and this the uncle agreed to do if the workhouse authorities would allow it. But Geordie was one of the most useful of the boys, and endless difficulties were placed in his way of escape.

At last, after many weary months of that greyest of lives in the workhouse, he gained his wish, and was, as he fondly fancied, free, and beginning the work that was to enable him to help his mother and sister.

The captain of the little vessel, however, for some reason, which seemed to all who knew Geordie at Shingleborough, quite incomprehensible, took a strong dislike to the lad (Geordie thought he wanted to take some nephew of his own), and used every opportunity of first giving him work he had never learnt to do, and then of beating him for not doing it properly.

---

[101] The Education Act 1870.

The vessel had one day to lie-to in a Yorkshire harbour for a few hours, just after one of those cruel 'hidings' or 'strappings,' as Geordie called them, and in the soreness of his little heart and body he forgot that his uncle would be his friend when he got back, and fairly bolted from the ship.

He was extremely fortunate in finding another vessel without more than a day's delay, and on board her he had endeared himself to all the other hands, by his bright obliging ways, his dancing, cooking, and music; and on board her, too, he met with his accident.

"But I don't mind that, mother, 'cause now I've got a mother again."

"What became of your own mother, though, man?" she asked. And he said the last he heard was that his father was dead, and his mother going to be married again, and very angry with him for leaving his uncle's ship.

As he told the tale, he was pulling to pieces a cherished accordion, with mother-o'-pearl keys, belonging to the eldest of the widow's sons, a very smart young yachtsman, now ashore, who had lent him his previous instrument that he might play them his favourite north-country air of 'She's o'er the barn floor,' and 'Get up and bar the door.' The small musician declared it was out of tune and he must cure it, and the kind young sailor actually trusted him, though he watched the process with half-concealed anxiety.

By-and-bye the boy triumphantly waved the re-constructed instrument aloft, and began briskly to play through his tune, in the middle of which in came, rather shyly, a young barrister, with a solitaire-board and marbles, to have a game with the invalid. When he had gone, a little boy came and brought some eggs laid by a special hen, whose produce was chiefly devoted to the sick of the place. This little boy had not seen Geordie before, and when he had heard the story, and seen the queer bandaged limb, it was too much for him; pain of his own he bore most bravely, but this other boy's suffering made him fairly cry; he was a very *little* boy. Then Geordie, who had no sort of awkwardness in his simple heart, gave his little visitor a sounding kiss, and the lads became fast friends for ever. Geordie's visitors were much entertained by him; he was so perfectly natural, and so pleased with every kind thought or little gift. One housemaid sewed in the evenings at a set of collars and handkerchiefs for him; one other poor woman made him socks; so by degrees his clothes were got ready, and he was at last himself again.

In honour of this event a tea was given to the widow, her sons and Geordie, including every one of the poorer people who had in any way helped during his illness. And before every one Geordie spoke up and said, "This is going to be my mother now, and I'm going to be her son and help to work for her, and I'm going to sea next month to earn some money."

No one thought him strong enough for the knock-about life on a fishing smack, but the widow's sons promised to take care of him, and at last he bade his 'mother' a proud good-bye and started gaily on a fishing cruise, only, alas! at the end of three weeks to be brought home with the same thigh broken in a different place – this time having been tripped up by a little dog. "So here I am, mother, back again, and not a penny earned yet," he said, bearing his pain most bravely, and giving less trouble than before.

When he first came to Shingleborough he was as ignorant of all religious knowledge as possible, but by this time he had learned a great deal, always with the greatest interest.

A lady gave him a very simple little book of separate prayers, and explained to him the way to make such prayers real and helpful, and I think there were few greater treasures in his possession than this little book, that so many boys would never have opened. He was immensely interested in St. Paul's shipwreck,[102] especially as he knew a port called Fair Havens, "where it was generally rather rough," he explained, and he honestly and

---

[102] Acts 27:14–44.

truly tried his best to be a good boy, especially after his second recovery.

The new schools were to be opened with a parochial tea on a night in November, and I had gone down to help in serving the guests, when Geordie arrived at our house to say good-bye; for in spite of all representations, he was off again to sea the next day.

He brought a large piece of jet, his own finding, as a present for me, and left an affectionate little farewell message, seeming very much disappointed at not seeing me.

Next day he went fishing, and when in the boat shooting cod-lines a violent and sudden squall arose, which drove the smack a long way from the boat, and overturned the latter. To scramble on its wrong side was not hard for the fishermen, and they helped up poor little Geordie, who was still rather stiff from his accident. There too they sat, getting dreadfully numb and cold, and almost hidden from the smack by the tremendous swell of the sea.

At last, by clever steering, she came within hailing distance, and they signed for ropes to be thrown. All they had were cod-lines, none too strong for the work, not the least for towing heavily-built heavy-clad men through a boiling sea. Yet it came to that, or death where they were, and what man would not sooner die in an effort to live, rather than be killed when merely waiting for death. One by one, three of the men swung themselves into the seething waters, each with a cod-line round his waist, and were safely dragged to the smack by the crew, but when it came to Geordie's turn his courage failed, and he dared not trust himself with his stiff leg to that slight cord, as it looked to him.

The other man who still remained on the bottom of the boat was a very large, handsome young fellow, named Harry Brown, a universal favourite, good-tempered, kindly, merry, with a great golden beard, and keen steel blue eyes. He had been married only the week before, after a long engagement, to a very nice woman, and life seemed to be at its best and fullest for him.

There were two of them, and only one cod-line left, and Geordie so helpless.

"Cheer up Geordie, man," the others heard Harry Brown say before they leaped into the sea. "If you've not heart enough to go alone, then we'll go together."

Geordie was too sensible not to see that the risk for two was greater than for one, and he said, "No, Harry, you go first and throw me a rope when you get there."

Harry would not hear of leaving him, bound the line round them both, plunged into the sea, and helped the men who were pulling in the line, as much as possible by his vigorous swimming. Suddenly, when the two were very near the smack, the wind veered again; a swish of water rushed over them. Geordie's white face was seen for one instant above the foam, then the rope relaxed in the smacksmen's hands, and they knew it was all over with Harry and Geordie.

The effort had been too much for the noble fellow, encumbered as he was with all his fisherman's clothes, and the weight of the fainting boy, and neither he nor Geordie were ever seen again, nor were their bodies washed ashore.

"Greater love hath no man than this, that he lay down his life for his friend."

The sad news soon reached the little town of Shingleborough, where there was not a single heart that did not grieve over the untimely deaths of the 'town's pet,' as they often called Geordie, and of the universal favourite Harry Brown, the young bridegroom.

His wife was worthy of her husband, for when she was told of her terrible loss and the way it had come about, she said, proudly, with a happy smile through her bitter tears, "I wouldn't have it otherwise; my Harry was right to try and save the boy."

Someone said carelessly, "Well, the boy was but a waif; no good to anyone, and Harry was a breadwinner."

Mrs. Brown turned sharply on the speaker, and answered, "Never say so again in my hearing. God sent us that boy to tend, and my Harry did well, and I'm proud to lose him so."

Then, poor woman, in her bitter sorrow, she went to see the widow, whose motherly heart had so enfolded the boy that she felt his death like the death of her own son, and the two women cried together and comforted one another.

The widow's son, the yachtsman, when he came home and heard the news, wept like a girl, and it was weeks before he could speak steadily of the little lad whose simply ways had so endeared him to every one who knew him.

A memorial card was painted for this man as a token of the deep sympathy felt for him, and his emotion at receiving it was most touching. Next time he came home he brought a tortoise to the painter, and whenever they met, his greeting is one of the most cordial she ever receives.

Little Geordie unconsciously did much good in that place; in the interest he aroused, all classes met on a common ground. In the unselfish kindness he drew out, people learned to think better of one another, and in the cheery patience with which he bore his two painful accidents, and his grateful, loving devotion to 'mother,' the children, who were his constant visitors, learned how much they had to be thankful for; their uneventful lives having before seemed just matters of course.

Bibliography

Adams, M., *In the Footsteps of Borrow and Fitzgerald* (London: Jarrold and Sons, 1914)

Bell, K., *The Magical Imagination: Magic and Modernity in Urban England, 1780–1914* (Cambridge: Cambridge University Press, 2012)

Chambers, R., *The Book of Days: A Miscellany of Popular Antiquities* (W. R. Chambers: London, 1862)

Briggs, K. (ed.), *An Encyclopedia of Fairies: Hobgoblins, Brownies, Bogies, and other Supernatural Creatures*, 2nd edn (New York: Pantheon, 1976)

Erckmann-Chatrian, M. M., *Hugues-le-Loup: Contes de la Montagne* (Paris: Levy, 1860)

'Folk-Lore Bibliography', Folklore 2:3 (September 1891), pp. 394–400

Forby, R., *The Vocabulary of East Anglia* (J. B. Nichols and Son: London, 1830), 2 vols

Gurdon, E. C. (ed.), *County Folk-lore Printed Extracts No. 2: Suffolk* (Ipswich: Pawsey and Hayes for The Folklore Society, 1893)

Hartsiotis, K., *Suffolk Folk Tales* (Stroud: The History Press, 2013)

Howitt, W. [and Howitt, M.], *The History of the Supernatural in All Ages and Nations* (London: Longman, Green, Longman, Roberts & Green, 1863), 2 vols

James, M. H., *Bogie Tales of East Anglia* (Ipswich: Pawsey & Hayes, 1891)

Jobson, A., *Under a Suffolk Sky* (London: Robert Hale, 1964)

Killip, M., *The Folklore of the Isle of Man* (London: Batsford, 1975)

Moor, E., *Bealings Bells: An Account of the Mysterious Ringing of Bells at Great Bealings, Suffolk, in 1834* (John Loder: Woodbridge, 1841)

Murray, J. (ed.), *Handbook for Essex, Suffolk, Norfolk and Cambridgeshire* (London: John Murray, 1870)

Newton, M., *Savage Girls and Wild Boys: A History of Feral Children*, 2nd edn (London: Faber and Faber, 2010)

Norgate, G. Le G. (rev. A. P. Baker), 'Boycott [*formerly* Boycatt], Charles Cunningham', *Oxford Dictionary of National Biography*, online edition, doi.org/10.1093/ref:odnb/3100

Pardoe, R., 'Queries', *The Ghosts & Scholars M. R. James Newsletter* 1 (March, 2002), online edition, users.globalnet.co.uk/~pardos/GSNews1.html

Pardoe, R., 'Miss M. H. James, author of *Bogie Tales of East Anglia*', *The Ghosts & Scholars M. R. James Newsletter* 31 (April, 2017), p. 32

Perrone, F. H., 'James, Minnie Stewart Rhodes (1863–1903)', *Oxford Dictionary of National Biography*, online edition, doi.org/10.1093/ref:odnb/59735

Porter, E., *Cambridgeshire Customs and Folklore* (London: Routledge and Kegan Paul, 1969)

Seccombe, T. (rev. J. B. Katz), 'Moor, Edward (1771–1848)', *Oxford Dictionary of National Biography*, online edition, doi.org/10.1093/ref:odnb/19089

Smith, A., *The Ghost Story, 1840–1920: A Cultural History* (Manchester: Manchester University Press, 2010)

Suckling, A., *The History and Antiquities of the County of Suffolk* (John Weale: London, 1846), 2 vols

Tolhurst, P., *This Hollow Land: Aspects of Norfolk Folklore* (Norwich: Black Dog Books, 2018)

Walsham, A., 'Invisible helpers: angelic intervention in post-Reformation England', *Past and Present* 208 (2010), pp. 77–130

Watson, S. F., 'Some Materials for a History of Printing and Publishing in Ipswich', *Proceedings of the Suffolk Institute of Archaeology and History* 24 (1948), pp. 182–227

Westwood, J., and Simpson, J., *The Lore of the Land: A Guide to England's Legends, from Spring-Heeled Jack to the Witches of Warboys* (London: Penguin, 2005)

Young, F., *Suffolk Fairylore* (Norwich: Lasse Press, 2018)

Index

Made in United States
North Haven, CT
01 August 2022